Purple Rain

D1547864

Series Editor: Barry Monush

OCT 2013

WI

Purple Rain

John Kenneth Muir

AN IMPRINT OF HAL LEONARD CORPORATION

Published in 2012 by Limelight Editions
An Imprint of Hal Leonard Corporation
7777 West Bluemound Road
Milwaukee, WI 53213

Trade Book Division Editorial Offices
33 Plymouth St., Montclair, NJ 07042

The photos on pages 3–5 and 8 of the insert are courtesy of Photofest. All other photos are from the author's personal collection.

Printed in the United States of America

Book design by Mark Lerner

Library of Congress Cataloging-in-Publication Data

Muir, John Kenneth, 1969-
 Purple rain / John Kenneth Muir.
    p. cm. -- (Music on film)
 Includes bibliographical references and index.
 ISBN 978-0-87910-396-5
1. Purple rain (Motion picture) 2. Musical films--History and criticism.
I. Title.
 PN1997.P886M85 2012
 791.43'6578--dc23

                            2012002293

www.limelighteditions.com

To my amazing mom, Loretta Muir,
with deepest love and affection

CONTENTS

ACKNOWLEDGMENTS

As always, a huge word of thanks goes to my enterprising literary agent, June Clark. Also, my special gratitude and appreciation goes out to *Purple Rain* director Albert Magnoli, producer Robert Cavallo, and assistant film editor Ken Robinson for participating in this retrospective and also for proving to be so much fun and so informative to speak with.

Purple Rain

CHAPTER 1

Baby I'm a Star
An Introduction

As Albert Magnoli's *Purple Rain* (1984) commences, the famous Warner Bros. logo appears onscreen. Accompanying the familiar crest-shaped icon, we hear an announcer's deep voice make a deadpan, serious introduction: "Ladies and gentlemen . . . the Revolution."

Applause and whistles of approval emanate from an unseen audience.

After a few seconds, we fade in on a solitary figure standing on a stage at the First Avenue Club in Minneapolis . . . dominating attention. "The Kid" (Prince) is silhouetted in the dead center of the frame, his hands gripping a guitar. Fog surrounds this unmoving stranger, a man stationed beneath a haze of red and blue strobe lights. But he doesn't move, gesticulate, or even sing, at least initially.

Instead, this guitar hero simply speaks . . . and the audience holds its collective breath, listening to and absorbing every last word of the monologue.

"Dearly beloved, we are gathered here today to get through this thing called life . . ." The Kid declares.

The imagery transmitted and also the words uttered during this inaugural cinematic moment instantly create a powerful sense of *mystery* about the celebrated star of this 1980s cinematic production, an early and dazzling MTV-era twist on and update of the long-established backstage musical format.

What about "this thing called life" can we understand as it relates to Prince and both his personal and professional stories? What human qualities can we ascribe to this character of rock royalty?

Or put more simply: Who, precisely, is this most singular and most enigmatic of music stars?

For many movie and music fans, *Purple Rain* offers some important answers, or at least hints at them. And the film's memorable opening salvo—a staccato burst of sound and fury; a rousing, seven-minute rendition of the celebratory tune "Let's Go Crazy"—represents the exact moment they first encountered and likely fell in love with the inscrutable, ultimately unknowable Prince.

The celebrated, Oscar-winning *Purple Rain* thus initiated in America (and in much of the rest of the world too) the so-called "Purple Age of Prince," as PBS TV host Tavis Smiley perfectly termed the epoch on one memorable occasion.

Yet more than twenty-five years later, an impossible full quarter century after Prince's rock 'n' roll silver screen debut, the artist remains—to a surprising and even unprecedented degree, given the modern world of new media, social networks, and reality television—that same inscrutable Kid standing semiobscured in the mist.

Prince is notoriously reclusive with the media, rarely granting interviews, but his albums have sold millions worldwide despite his silence. Additionally, the artist seems to take little career counsel beyond his own, and even his storied familial background remains cloaked in shadows, mystery, and contradictions.

So Prince has brilliantly "established himself as an adventurous artist and a showman of rare energy"[1]; simultaneously, he indelibly remains what one critic termed a "polyamorous changeling."[2] The same critic describes musical influences on Prince as diverse as Jimi Hendrix, James Brown, and Joni Mitchell.

Prince remains, in fact, a mass of personal and professional contradictions. Writing for *The Nation* in 1984, film critic Andrew Kopkind spelled out the strange Prince mystique with crystal clarity. "His costume changes run from the itsiest bikini to Edwardian overdress. He is tender and tough, S&M, straight and gay, First World and Third, coal black, lily white and deep purple."[3]

Music historians would likely add to that tally the fact that the man is an acknowledged "musical genius," and a virtual one-man band "with the ability to play twenty-three instruments."[4] They would similarly note, perhaps, that Prince played a crucial leadership role in crafting what is now known as "the Minneapolis Sound," a "highly textured blend of melodic pop and gritty funk with shrill synthesizers and heavy drumbeat."[5]

Not everyone appreciates Prince and his contradictions, mind you. He's made powerful enemies: conservatives and religious fundamentalists have termed him "the filthiest rock 'n' roller ever to prance across the stage,"[6] despite his oft-stated Christian belief and faith in God. No less than Tipper Gore—once nearly America's First Lady—launched a campaign in the mid-1980s against rock lyrics based almost entirely on her personal experience listening to Prince's ribald *Purple Rain* hit, "Darling Nikki."

Yet the women in his life have repeatedly avowed Prince's core decency and chivalry. Apollonia, whom Prince once managed musically as the lead singer of Apollonia 6, has noted, for instance, his "heart of gold."[7] When you gaze across the spectrum of female music stars Prince has helped launch, from Vanity and Apollonia to Sheila E. and Sinead

O'Connor, his professional generosity and guidance can't be easily denied.

So Prince is a music superstar *and* a recluse; he's a charismatic motion-picture leading man, *and* he's just 5'5" tall (or 5'2" depending on the source). He's a clean-living, hardworking, "verbally conservative"[8] (meaning taciturn) rock 'n' roller known for his vegetarianism, his religious faith, and even his hard stance against Warner Bros., the benefactor that first signed him to a million-dollar contract in 1977 and that Prince later equated with a slaveholder.

Recently, *Purple Rain* celebrated its twenty-fifth anniversary as a pop-culture landmark, an MTV-era "backstage musical" from the heyday of *Flashdance* (1983), *Staying Alive* (1983), *Footloose* (1984), *Hard to Hold* (1984), and other representatives of the form. Looking back, the film still appears the intrepid Prince fan's last, best hope for understanding something personal, intimate, and true about this unusual musical individual.

Albert Magnoli and William Blinn's semiautobiographical story about band infighting, personal chaos, and a violent, unpredictable home life in Minneapolis, marred by domestic abuse, seems to take much from Prince's real life story, while inventing or augmenting certain aspects of his biography. This is the movie that "propelled Prince into the cultural mainstream" and for many remains a "revealing artifact."[9]

Today, Prince has receded largely into that mist he first stepped out of in *Purple Rain*, as mysterious and unknowable as ever, having once changed his name to an unpronounceable symbol and making grave pronouncements about the future of the Internet, for instance, in summer 2010.

Yet the 1984 movie remains extant: a living, breathing testament to his enduring talent and appeal, as well as the dedication of the men and women who had the audacity and know-how to imagine the artist as a full-fledged 1980s movie star, contradictions and all.

Admirably, the movie yet serves as both a rock star's "mixed-up confession" and the requisite "self-glorifying fantasy"[10] we've come to expect from the rock movie tradition, according to film critic David Denby. In other words, it tells the truth . . . but *not too much*, perhaps. For in the body of the film, lest we forget it, Prince is not Prince alone. He is also "The Kid," a figure as glowering and mysterious as Clint Eastwood's Man with No Name.

Purple Rain has been hailed as the greatest rock movie ever made. It has been termed the *Citizen Kane* of rock movies on many occasions, by Roger Ebert in his review of *Sign 'o' the Times* (1987) and others. Prince's screen presence has been likened to no less than that of Marlon Brando in *The Wild One* (1953).

However, the 1984 Prince film has also been minimized as a "delicious slice of '80s nostalgia that is absolutely indecipherable to anyone who wasn't actually there."[11] I'm not certain this is true, since *Purple Rain* is erected on a solid foundation of proven film grammar, plus some of the best pop music of the 1980s.

With a bit of timely assistance from *Purple Rain*'s energetic director, Albert Magnoli; producer, Robert Cavallo; and assistant editor, Ken Robinson, this book recalls in detail the history, making, and legacy of *Purple Rain*. In so many crucial ways, this film represents Prince at his most identifiable, his most human, and his most *approachable*, and for those reasons alone, it is a valuable document, a time capsule of his career.

More importantly, however, it's a sturdy, visually dazzling movie, one that evokes excitement, sympathy, and in the end, affection. So with all that in mind, let's go crazy all over again.

CHAPTER 2

If You Just Believed in Me
The Story of *Purple Rain*

Purple Rain is an unconventional backstage musical, one that offers a warts-and-all peek behind the curtain, so to speak, revealing the real-life cycle of violence and insecurity behind the talent of a remarkable Minneapolis musician enigmatically known as "The Kid" (Prince).

At the First Avenue Club in Minneapolis, "The Kid" performs with his bandmates in the Revolution, including Wendy (Wendy Melvoin) and Lisa (Lisa Coleman), who desperately want him to make use of their musical writing contributions too. "The Kid" resists. Meanwhile, he deals with domestic abuse at home from his father (Clarence Williams III), a failed musician who thinks that his wife (Olga Karlatos) no longer "believes in him" and tells her that he would "die for" her.

When a lovely and ambitious young woman, Apollonia (Apollonia Kotero), arrives in town, her alluring presence and burning desire to "make it" in the music world ups the competitive relationship between "The Kid" and another First Avenue Club performer, the charismatic, smug dandy Morris E. Day (Morris Day) of the group the Time.

"The Kid" falls hard for Apollonia, but steadfastly refuses to help her become a success in the business. And after "The Kid" slaps Apollonia for what he perceives as a major betrayal—just like his old man—she goes running into the grip of Day and his sidekick Jerome (Jerome Benton), who use her to head a sexy new group called Apollonia 6 that debuts at another club, The Taste.

Finally, Billy Sparks (himself) the manager of the nightclub, informs "The Kid" that he now has more than enough acts for the venue, so unless he can turn things around, the Revolution will be squeezed out to make room for Apollonia 6.

After his father's attempted suicide at home, "The Kid" examines his life, his personal and professional choices, and the wide-open road ahead. In what might be his last performance at the First Avenue Club, he decides to make a clean break with the past. He dedicates a song—Wendy and Lisa's song, "Purple Rain"—to his father, and brings the house down.

Purple Rain (1984)

THE CREDITS

Producers: Robert Cavallo, Joseph Ruffalo, Steven Fargnoli

Director: Albert Magnoli

Screenplay: William Blinn, Albert Magnoli

Original Songs Composer and Producer: Prince

Additional Music: Michel Columbier, John L. Nelson

Production Designer: Ward Preston

First Assistant Directors: Anthony Brand, Britt Lomond

Director of Photography: Donald Thorin

Costume Designer: Marie France

Film Editors: Albert Magnoli, Ken Robinson

Casting: David Graham

Set Decoration: Anne McCulley

Make-up: Richard Arrington

Sound Editors: James Beshears, Bruce Bisenz, Mike Dobie

Stunt Coordinator: Al Jones

Technicolor

111 Minutes

Rated R

Cavallo, Ruffalo and Fargnoli present Prince in *Purple Rain*.

Released through Warner Bros.

THE CAST

The Kid...Prince
Apollonia ....Apollonia Kotero
Morris E. Day...Morris Day
Mother .... Olga Karlatos
Father .... Clarence Williams III
Jerome .... Jerome Benton
Billy ....Billy Sparks
Jill ....Jill Jones
Chick... Charles Huntsberry
Dez .... Dez Dickerson
Brenda..Brenda Bennett
Susan ....Susan Moonsie
Beautiful Babe ....Sandra Clark Gershman
Kim...Kim Upsher
Stagehand ....Alan Leeds
Taste M.C..Israel Gordon
Cop ....Gil Jacobson
First Avenue M.C. .... Joseph A. Ferraro
Cabbie ....James French
Wendy .... Wendy Melvoin
Lisa .... Lisa Coleman
Bobby Z..Bobby Z. Rivkin
Brown... Brown Mark

Matt ....Matt Fink
Mark...Mark Cardenas
Paul... Paul Peterson

THE SONGS (IN ORDER OF APPEARANCE)

"Let's Go Crazy"
Words and music by Prince
Performed by Prince and the Revolution

"Jungle Love"
Words and music by Morris Day and Jesse Johnson
Performed by Morris Day and the Time

"Take Me with U"
Words and music by Prince
Performed by Prince and Apollonia

"Modernaire"
Words and music by Dez Dickerson
Performed by Dez Dickerson

"The Beautiful Ones"
Words and music by Prince
Performed by Prince

"God" (Love Theme from *Purple Rain*)
Composed and performed by Prince

"When Doves Cry"
Words and music by Prince
Performed by Prince

"Computer Blue"
Words and music by Wendy Melvoin, Lisa Coleman, and
    Prince
Performed by Prince

"Darling Nikki"
Words and music by Prince
Performed by Prince

"Sex Shooter"
Words and music by Apollonia 6 and The Starr Company
Performed by Apollonia 6

"The Bird"
Words and music by Morris Day and Jesse Johnson
Performed by Morris Day and the Time

"Purple Rain"
Words and music by Prince
Performed by Prince and the Revolution

"I Would Die 4 U"
Words and music by Prince
Performed by Prince and the Revolution

"Baby I'm a Star"
Words and music by Prince
Performed by Prince and the Revolution

THE CRITICAL ROUND-UP

"Director Albert Magnoli, making his feature bow, gets a solid, appealing performance from Prince, whose sensual, somewhat androgynous features are as riveting on film as they are on a concert stage."—Cynthia Kirk, "*Purple Rain,*" *Variety,* July 3, 1984

"*Purple Rain,* which introduces Prince, the rising young rock performer, to theatrical films, is probably the flashiest album cover ever to be released as a movie. However, like many album covers, *Purple Rain*, though sometimes arresting to look at, is a cardboard come-on to the record it contains." —Vincent Canby, "*Purple Rain,*" *The New York Times,* July 27, 1984

"The film is like *East of Eden* replayed as a hyperbolic rock fever dream."—Owen Gleiberman, *Entertainment Weekly,* September 21, 1990

"*Purple Rain* sets a dynamic new standard for the marriage of contemporary pop and movies that so many ambitious musicians will fail to match, including Prince, who'll go on to make three more films."—Nelson Greg, *Post Soul Nation: The Explosive, Contradictory, Triumphant and Tragic 1980s as Experienced by African-Americans* (New York: Penguin Group, 2005), 93

"The picture . . . is a time capsule of style and attitude. It does what musicals are supposed to do: it rides the underlying currents of its moment and renders them glorious."—Mick La Salle, "*Purple Rain* Captures a Distinctly '80s Dream: Silly Film Still Has Style, Fresh Music," *The San Francisco Chronicle,* January 1, 1999

CHAPTER 3

I Want Some Perfection
The Making of the Movie

This is . . . Prince?

Named after his father's jazz band, the Prince Rogers Trio, the rock artist sometimes known as Prince arrived in this thing called life on June 7, 1958. His parents were John Nelson and Mattie Shaw of Minneapolis, Minnesota.

A child of divorce, reportedly nicknamed "Skipper," Prince grew up poor . . . but driven and immensely talented. After his parents split, he moved in with an aunt for a time, but then settled down in the household of his best friend's mother, Bernadette Anderson.

As a child, Prince devoted his energies to music, both singing in a church choir and teaching himself to play on the piano the catchy theme songs to sixties TV series

like *Batman* (1966–1968) and *The Man from U.N.C.L.E.*
(1964–1968).

Prince has remembered in conversations with Oprah
Winfrey and print journalists the experience of being teased
at school as a child and young man, and feeling isolated
from his classmates during his stint at Minneapolis Central.

Precocious from the start, Prince reportedly composed
his first original song at the tender age of seven, a piece
titled "Funk Machine."[1] He joined a rock band called Grand
Central (later, Champagne) in 1972, while he was still in
high school. Members of Prince's first band included the
irrepressible Morris Day, a costar in *Purple Rain* and front
man for the Time.

Prince has cited a James Brown concert he saw at age
ten (with his stepfather) as one of his seminal musical influences.[2] He also has recalled watching early Jackson 5 TV
appearances and being inspired by them, as well as by the
music of Stevie Wonder.

By age sixteen, Prince had left school and was toiling
in a Minneapolis band called Flyte Tyme with drummer
Jellybean Johnson and bassist Terry Lewis. But everything
changed in 1976. After playing in guitar sessions with Pepe
Willie at Sound 80 Studios in Minneapolis, Prince prepared a
demo tape with sound engineer Chris Moon. His efforts met
with great interest from a local Minneapolis entrepreneur,

Owen Husney. Husney then formed a musician management company and helped Prince revise his scintillating sound for a new, improved demo tape (for which Husney also footed the bill).[3]

It wasn't long before young Prince appeared on the radar of Warner Bros., and the rest, as they say, is history. Prince's rise in the industry might accurately be termed meteoric, despite setbacks such as being booed off the stage when opening for the Rolling Stones. That notorious incident occurred in San Francisco in 1981, and a "sizable minority of the crowd chose to hurl anything from shoes to a bag of chicken innards" at the young star on the rise.[4]

In terms of Prince's much talked-about personal background, it has long been rumored that he came from an abusive household and that his father beat his mother; some sources have suggested this is not exactly the case, and that talk of abuse has been exaggerated or played up. In magazines published at the time of *Purple Rain*'s release, Prince and his father both reported a good, friendly relationship, based largely on their mutual love and affinity for music and music composition. In fact, some of these periodical accounts suggested Prince and his father literally composed identical songs.

This biographical material is relevant to the film *Purple Rain* and this book only inasmuch as the film has largely been read by critics and audiences as an accurate biography of the star, not merely of the character he plays.

"It Can't Be a Jeweler or a Drug Dealer That Cavallo Knows . . ."

By the late 1970s, Prince had begun to really hone his musical persona and style, not to mention attract a fervent following. By 1979, he had released the albums *For You* and the self-titled *Prince*. The latter effort shot up the charts and went platinum, featuring such hits as "Why You Wanna Treat Me So Bad" and "I Wanna Be Your Lover."

Prince's fan base exploded in 1982 after a guest appearance on NBC's *Saturday Night Live* (1975–present), and in 1983 with the success of the album *1999*. In particular, the single "Little Red Corvette" reached number six on the U.S. charts, and "1999" topped out at number twelve.

Yet even with this early and significant success in the music industry, the enterprising young artist had not fulfilled at least one crucial career aspiration. Specifically, Prince had not yet headlined a rock 'n' roll film in the grand tradition of Elvis, the Beatles, or even the Bee Gees. He was acutely aware of the opportunities offered by Hollywood, and for years previous to production of his first film, he kept a (legendarily) purple notebook on hand during tours and performances in which he assiduously scrawled notes about possible movie ideas and sequences.

"Prince was fascinated with the camera," Bobby Z, a member of Prince's band, the Revolution, told Prince chronicler and biographer Per Nilsen about those days. "We were always videotaping rehearsals and shows. We were also making skits. He was always talking about doing a movie."[5]

Prince reportedly viewed making a film as a "new mountain to climb, a new challenge, a new stimulus."[6] More than that, author Matthew Carcieri, who penned *Prince: A Life in Music*, noted that "Prince loved the movies and seemed to have a healthy appreciation for the medium's power to subvert popular culture. A film would be the perfect vessel for bottling his image-heavy vision. It would be his final, full-frontal assault."[7]

The story of *Purple Rain*'s production and Prince's entrée into the universe of movies begins with this ambitious desire for silver screen fame, and some seed money from Warner Bros. Records, courtesy of a supportive, artist-friendly individual named Mo Ostin (1927–), a man renowned in the industry for signing Jimi Hendrix, Paul Simon, Neil Young, and The Red Hot Chili Peppers to contracts. When Ostin signed off on the idea of a Prince movie there was no music, no script—just a sense of great unexplored potential.

To begin to fully realize that potential, it took the herculean efforts of a legendary, storied producer named Robert Cavallo. Today, the gentlemanly and laconic Cavallo serves as Chairman of the Buena Vista Music Group at Walt Disney Corp. But after graduating from Georgetown University in Washington, D.C., he held a number of diverse jobs, including taxi driver and bank employee. He also managed a triumvirate of hip nightclubs in D.C. for a time.

But then, he broached another career.

"Eventually I had three joints," Mr. Cavallo told me during an interview in late summer 2010, "and I sold out, went to New York—which is where I was from—and started a management company managing the Lovin' Spoonful. They had ten top-ten records in a row, so I was off to the races," he explained. "Then I signed Earth, Wind and Fire in 1970, and Little Feat and Weather Report.

"Then, in 1979, I signed Prince."

Employed at Cavallo's management company were two junior partners, Joe Ruffalo and Steve Fargnoli. Together, this triumvirate helped to drive the direction and shape of Prince's career in the early years.

"We did a really good job managing him for the first five years," Cavallo reflected. "And when it was time to get a new contract, Prince was on the road and young Steve was out on tour with him. I called him and I said, 'Steve, I'm sending you a blank contract. I'd like to see if we can get Prince to sign up for another five.'"

Prince had an answer ready for that request, but it wasn't one that the managers expected. At all. Steve Fargnoli returned Cavallo's call a "few days later," according to Cavallo, and said, "'You're not going to believe this, Bob, but he'll resign with us'—we did a decent job—'but only if we get him a motion picture.'"

In addition, Prince reportedly had a set of very specific terms about the nature and shape of that prospective motion picture—or more accurately, how it would be financed, sponsored, and presented.

"It had to have Prince's name above the title and it had to be with a major studio," Cavallo said. Prince apparently also specified that the movie couldn't be funded by "one of those jewelers or drug dealers that Cavallo knows."

"I don't know any drug dealers!" Cavallo stresses with good humor. "But anyway, that's what he said. It had to be a real, big-time movie. And I went, 'Oh my god,' and then we went about the search [to find a writer]."

Cavallo contacted his lawyer, Harry "Skip" Brittenham, a senior partner in Ziffren Brittenham, LLLP, founded in 1978. Brittenham then connected Cavallo with the award-winning writer William Blinn, who had authored teleplays for TV series as diverse as *Gunsmoke* (1955–1975), *Starsky and Hutch* (1975–1979), and *Eight Is Enough* (1977–1981).

Perhaps Blinn remains most well known for writing episodes of the watershed miniseries *Roots* (1977) and the 1971 TV movie *Brian's Song*. At the time he became involved with the Prince movie project, Blinn was executive producing the TV series *Fame* (1982–1987).

The author developed an outline for his script and traveled to Minneapolis in March 1983 to meet Prince and discuss the details. The two men had several false starts getting together, and Blinn nearly left the project, apparently fearing he was dealing with a typical capricious rock star. Finally, he and Prince met, and based on their discussion, Blinn wrote a script about a young musician grappling with life and death. The story reportedly featured heavy violence and even a murder-suicide involving the lead character's troubled parents.

"I went to Hollywood, where Prince was putting together final touches on a video," Blinn told *Spin Magazine*'s Brian Raftery in 2009. "Met him at an Italian restaurant in Hollywood. What I remembered more than anything was that he was the only person I had ever seen in my life who had pasta and orange drink. I didn't get it then, I don't get it now, but what the hell. He had definite ideas of what he wanted to do—a generalized story line, broad strokes. It wasn't his life, but it was about his life. Not that it was wall-to-wall docudrama, but he knew where he'd come from, and he wanted the movie to reflect that."[8]

"He was a writer who won an Emmy, and I wanted a movie writer," explained Cavallo about Blinn's participation, "but it [the movie] didn't seem interesting to movie people. William did a wonderful job. Then we went about the process of trying to get directors, and I failed on every level. Every director passed." In fact, according to Cavallo, *Purple Rain* was eventually "turned down by every director in the guild."

At a loss—and with Prince's contract absolutely on the line—Cavallo kept up the search as best he could. His next lead for a director emerged from a surprise meeting with a promising young filmmaker.

Enter Albert Magnoli: *Purple Rain* Gets a Director

"I saw a movie called *Reckless* (1984), in a screening room, which was done by Jamie Foley," Robert Cavallo explains. That cult film was a rebellious rock 'n' roll anthem featuring Aidan Quinn and Daryl Hannah as star-crossed lovers in an American steel town, and it featured a pulsing, hard-rock soundtrack from the likes of INXS, Bob Seger, and Romeo Void.

"I was alone in the screening room, other than a young man sitting in the back," Cavallo says. "As I walked out, the young man said to me, 'Well, what did you think?' And I said, 'It was pretty good . . . but I especially enjoyed the editing.' I wasn't kidding. It was good. I thought it was really well edited," Cavallo emphasizes. "And he said, 'Oh, I did that. Jamie's my friend; he made the movie, and I was the editor. We went to USC film school.'"

That young man was Albert Magnoli, a native of Connecticut and a recent graduate of USC School of Cinematic Arts (until 2006 named the School of Cinema-Television). He had discovered his interest in film during undergraduate school, and almost unexpectedly.

"I grew up in New England, in Connecticut, and in undergraduate school, I took a course—I was a literature major—that pretty much changed my life," Mr. Magnoli remembered. "It was a course that dealt with the films of Ingmar Bergman and how they related to literature; Bergman in relation to stories and novels. The professor was extremely good at finding comparisons between Ingmar Bergman's philosophies and the philosophies of Kierkegaard, Dostoyevsky, etc.

"We tracked Ingmar Bergman from the 1950s all the way to, at that time, the 1970s, and that was an extremely rich time for Ingmar Bergman," Magnoli reminisces. "He started off doing romantic comedies and then concentrated on films that dealt with his background and religious philosophy.

We watched *The Seventh Seal* (1957), *Persona* (1966), *Shame* (1968), and *Cries and Whispers* (1972) and they just had an enormous impact on me.

"What ended up happening was, there was a film course being offered in the school. I wasn't part of it, but someone in the course came to me and asked if I had any short stories that could be turned into a short film," the director says. "At the time I was writing short stories, and said I had one, and gave it to him. The location of that story needed a factory, and I had worked in a factory during the summer months, so I said, 'I have a factory, and it's down in Newington. I'll talk to the manager and see if he'll let us film in there.' And sure enough, he did. He let us film from midnight till six a.m.

"We had one night to do it," Magnoli details. "So I brought my friend and his crew to this factory. We were all juniors in college at the time. And when we got there, he looked at me and said, 'Where should the camera go?'"

"I said, 'I thought this was your film class!' And he said, 'I'm just the choreographer, not the director. You know the factory—just tell me where to put the camera.' I said, 'Well, let me see what the camera looks like.' It was a little super 8 camera on a tripod. I looked through the viewfinder, and at that point I knew where the camera should go. And then I started setting up shots. Essentially, we filmed for the next five or six hours. We had our actors, we finished, and as I was riding back to college, I said to my friend, 'This is very interesting.'"

The next part of the process was even more interesting for Magnoli: the editing. Magnoli's friend had a "little super 8 viewer and editor, and he showed me how the technology worked, and very quickly I just said, 'Cut here, cut here, do this, do that.' We put it together very quickly."

From this surprise beginning in student films, Magnoli was accepted to USC and began the rigorous process of training to become a film director.

By 1983 and his encounter with Robert Cavallo in that screening room, Magnoli was a working film editor, and on Hollywood's radar because of his widely recognized, award-winning student film, *Jazz* (1979).

So Magnoli graciously offered to take Blinn's script for *Purple Rain*—then titled *Dreams*—to his friend James Foley. Cavallo was excited about the prospect, believing Foley could really do a good job with the material. For his part, Magnoli was happy that another film project seemed to be shaping up.

"I called Jamie up immediately and I said, 'We have our next picture. You'll direct and I'll edit. *Life is good*,'" Magnoli relates. "He said, 'Send me the script,' so I sent it to him, and he called me the next day and said, 'Are you out of your mind?'"

Life? *Not so good.*

In other words, James Foley—like the plethora of film directors before him—passed on the opportunity to bring Prince to the silver screen. But at least Foley did help the frustrated Cavallo find a director. He recommended that Prince's lead manager hire Magnoli himself.

At first Cavallo was intrigued; then, upon screening Magnoli's student film, *Jazz*, he was highly enthusiastic. The twenty-four-minute movie had been made as a thesis project while Magnoli was at film school and had won a Student Academy Award. In fact, the 1983 edition of *The Encyclopedia Britannica* listed *Jazz* as "the most honored student film made in this country in the last twenty years."[9]

"It was magnificent. You should see it," Cavallo enthuses. "I said, 'Wow, this guy can shoot music. I'm going to go hire him.'" He screened the student film for Prince, who also signed off on the choice of Magnoli as director.

But then Magnoli actually read the script for the film as written by Blinn and wasn't impressed. "It really didn't work. I was distressed and depressed," he exclaims.

So Magnoli followed Foley's example, according to Cavallo, and also passed on a directorship. His first directorship, actually.

"I said, 'How can you pass?'" recalls Cavallo with exasperation. "*How the fuck can you pass?* You don't have a pot to piss in, and I'm going to get you DGA minimum!"

Cavallo recalls, in particular, that Magnoli felt the script was "just too square."

"My recollection might be wrong about this, because I only looked at the script once, but there was very little music in it," Magnoli details. "I mean, it wasn't a musical. It was more of a . . . *I don't know what.*

"You actually see that a lot with musical artists," he muses. "The first thing they say is, 'I don't want to do music.' They don't want to be pinned with that musical label . . . they want to show that they have range. It's a knee-jerk reaction a lot of these artists have, but it's normal. I don't think there's anything abnormal about it. But it's not looking at the whole picture, because their core audience wants to see them sing and dance. So there's some friction there. . . ."

At that juncture, a desperate Cavallo urged Magnoli to change, tweak, and toy with the story as he saw fit; to create his own version of the narrative. Magnoli agreed. He called Cavallo and said they should get together to talk about it.

When Cavallo and Magnoli later met at Du Pars restaurant in the San Fernando Valley to discuss the film and Magnoli's involvement, the young prospective director offered up a new story that he had devised, one that felt more authentic.

"So when I sat down with Bob Cavallo at that breakfast meeting, I pitched him a whole new story on the spot," Magnoli explains. "I just took what in my gut felt right, and the funny thing about what I had pitched that morning—and what I eventually pitched to Prince after meeting him—was [it was] essentially a story that had no knowledge of what Prince himself was like.

"I hesitated for about two seconds and then launched into a story line that just came out of nowhere," Magnoli remembered. "It was the bare bones of *Purple Rain*. I even had the father writing music and hiding it. The family angle was in there because I've always been oriented toward the family angle. So I knew the father was angry and embittered and putting that energy into his kid, and Prince was combating it. I pretty much had [all] three acts."

And Magnoli had unknowingly made good guesses about his leading man's background. "The fact that Cavallo responded so avidly suggested that I was somewhat correct," Magnoli suggests.

Bob Cavallo concurs that in that meeting Magnoli "basically tells me the movie you saw." And the presentation of that stirring tale wasn't something he would soon forget, either.

"He's a very athletic guy," Cavallo describes. "He was squatting in the aisle, jumping up and down, emphasizing points physically, right there in the deli. It was very exciting." As he described the pitch and his own response, Cavallo almost ended up cheering at the end of it.

In particular, Cavallo recalls the young man's introductory flourish. "He said, 'Here's how we open the movie. Did you see the last scene in *The Godfather*? Do you remember when Michael's son is being christened, and we go back and forth to that and all his enemies being killed?'

"'Well, instead we'll have Prince opening the movie with a song. He's performing his first act, but we keep cutting back and forth to Prince getting his makeup on, and his band coming in, and Vanity hustling some taxi driver to get to this mecca for her future, and to Morris Day grooming himself . . .'

"And while he's doing this," Cavallo elaborates, "I'm hearing 'Let's Go Crazy.' And so, you know, I just thought . . . *that's the greatest idea ever*. And he made it a much harder-edged movie. So I hired him."

Meeting His Majesty, Prince

The next task at hand was to introduce Magnoli to Prince, and simultaneously, for Magnoli to further familiarize himself with the artist, his background, and his works. Magnoli knew and had liked the 1982 Prince hit singles "1999" and "Little Red Corvette." He held a powerful image of the artist as "a loner" and "iconoclastic," but more research was still necessary to get an authentic feel for the man and the performer.

So, while he finished an editing job on a Wednesday and Thursday and prepared for a flight to Minneapolis on Friday to meet his movie's star, Magnoli wanted to learn everything he could about the musician. "I didn't know his early career," Magnoli acknowledged.

"'Send to the editing room every video and any footage you have on Prince, so I can see the visuals,'" Magnoli remembers saying to Cavallo on the phone. "So he sent me all of this video of Prince in concert in Minneapolis, and it was during his bikini-wearing, high-heel wearing, long coat days. This was prior to the *1999* album, where I think he had his self-titled album *Prince* . . . I think that's what it was called. He was wearing a jacket on the cover [of the album] with a bikini bottom, with his chest sticking out, looking very androgynous.

"So now I'm watching all this video that supports this androgyny, and I'm thinking, *Wow . . . okay. . . .* I realized trying to bring Prince to the public—and I always knew I wanted to cross over from an urban base to a wider one—was going to be difficult," Magnoli explains.

"So I'm watching all this imagery, but I do see the vulnerability under all that crap, and I think, *Okay, I need to focus on that*," he notes. "That's where this is coming from anyway."

An encounter on the way to the airport didn't exactly quell Magnoli's concern that the visuals surrounding Prince might have difficulty playing in Peoria. He asked his African American cab driver on the way to LAX if he knew of the performer/songwriter Prince. The man did know of him, so Magnoli next pressed the gentleman on what he thought about him.

The man replied that Prince was gay, and furthermore, couldn't imagine that Prince was not gay.

"Don't forget," admonishes Magnoli, "we're back in 1983 now. Nowadays it's not even an issue. *We've come a long way, baby*. But now I'm thinking, *All right . . . more . . . stuff*. But when I later met him, I realized, no, this is not even an issue. This is just the noise. This is just the chatter. I never factored it in, ever—*ever*—from that point on. The frills didn't bother me. The purple coats didn't bother me. This was all the stuff, all the chatter, that anybody who didn't know the soul would just latch on to. And they were going to do that anyway. As long as I could stay focused on the heart and soul, I knew I would be fine."

When Magnoli arrived in Minneapolis late in the evening, he met Steve Fargnoli, who promptly informed him that his new story was off and the Blinn story was back on. Fargnoli—whom Magnoli sometimes jokingly referred to as "the second part of a three-part series," approached him with grave seriousness.

"The first words out of his mouth are: 'Understand this: I don't give a damn about the story you told Bob [Cavallo]. We're doing the story that's already written.' And I said, 'Uh huh.'"

Then Magnoli was taken to actually meet with Prince. In a hotel lobby, Magnoli first met Chick, Prince's legendary, Nordic bodyguard, whom Magnoli described as a very "tall, Viking-looking person," and then went off to a corner to observe the dynamics of the situation.

"To my right were the elevator doors," Magnoli explains. "To my left, across the lobby, was the front door of the building, where Steve [Fargnoli] and Chick were positioned. Then the doors opened at the crack of midnight sharp and out walks Prince by himself.

"Because he didn't know who I was, he didn't see me. He saw Chick and Steve at the end of the hall and walked to them, which allowed me to do a right-to-left pan with Prince, unencumbered by him knowing I was looking at him. As a result, I ended up filling [in] the whole story based on him walking across the lobby. Because what I saw was extreme vulnerability, in spite of all the bluster and the costume and the music. This was a vulnerable young man. I saw all the heart and soul. I saw all the emotional stuff. I saw the tragedy of his upbringing. I just saw stuff and felt stuff that filled in the three-act story."

Together, Prince, Magnoli, Cavallo, Fargnoli, and Chick went to a working dinner. "I was looking at Prince and I could tell he didn't like being looked at," Magnoli says. "He's very shy. Everybody ordered food, and as soon as the waitress left, Prince looked at me and said, 'Okay, how did you like my script?'

"I realized a few things there. One, he said, 'my script,' which meant that he had personally invested himself in whatever it was that William Blinn had written. And two, that he hadn't been told anything that I felt about it."

"The words that came out of my mouth were the following: 'Well, I think it sucked.'"

Magnoli pauses for dramatic effect. "At that moment, Steve dropped his head, Chick leaned closer to me, and Prince looked startled. Then I could see him thinking and what he was thinking was: 'I wasn't told this before this meeting was to take place. *Why wasn't I told?*' Then he looked toward Steve, because obviously Steve had told him nothing. That look to Steve took about three seconds, but it was telling to me, because now I saw how the operation worked. He had been kept in the dark about this."

"So then Prince looked back to me and said, 'Why does it suck?' And I said, 'You know what, it's not important why, but here's what we can do about it. Let me tell you the story.' So now, with even more passion, because I have more information now that I'm looking at this kid, I told this story.

"There was five seconds of silence. Then he looked at Steve and said, 'Why don't you take Chick and go home.' Then he looked at me and said, 'Why don't you come with me?' 'I'm just going to take Al for a ride.'"

Not knowing exactly what was going to happen, Magnoli remembers feeling a little uncertain. Had he offended Prince? Had he made him angry?

"We got in his car; he got behind the wheel, I got into the passenger's seat, and he took off fast," Magnoli notes. "The next thing I knew, we were driving in pitch-black darkness, [with] not a light in sight. I had no idea where we were. It looked like we were driving in a black tube. A day later I realized we were in horizon-to-horizon farmland, but there were no lights. So I was thinking, *He didn't like the story . . . and now I'm dead. I can die right now. and no one will know. . . .*"

This nighttime ride was not the beginning of a murder plot, however, but the start of a very fruitful working relationship for Magnoli and Prince. Even though the story Magnoli had recounted involved the lead character (Prince himself, hereafter called "The Kid") being at odds with his parents, his bandmates, and even his girlfriend, Prince never once flinched from a warts-and-all, three-dimensional presentation.

"The thing about Prince is that he wasn't concerned about his image," Magnoli reveals. "He was concerned about whether the film would communicate. Would the music communicate?

"I said to him, 'If you're willing to let me have your father in the movie give you a kick in the face on a certain page and get thrown across the room—if you're willing to take that hit—we can make a great movie.'

"And he said, 'I'm willing to take that hit.' So that was it, *metaphorically, realistically, and literally.* Because he does get smacked by his old man in the movie.

"And then I jokingly said to him, 'There isn't a person on the planet who wouldn't want to hit a rock star in the face,'" Magnoli continues. "And he laughed and said he understood that. We both understood that the image of these people as entitled and selfish was a target. We understood that.

"We never discussed warts and all. It just became part of the script and it was totally embraced," Magnoli explains.

When interviewed some time later, Prince reflected on the seemingly biographical aspects of the Magnoli script. "We used parts of my past and present to make the story pop more, but it was a story," he emphasized.[10]

Prepping *Purple Rain*

With Prince on board and approving of Magnoli's story line, it was time for Magnoli to actually settle down and write the script. "I had the meeting with Prince in June, I believe, and I still had commitments to *Reckless*, editorially," he described. "I had August off, and I went to Minneapolis."

For Magnoli, the time spent in the city authoring the script was glorious. He remembers a feeling of "writing with an independent spirit," far away from Hollywood and the business and any financial concerns of the studio.

"I only had eight days of research because I needed to start writing right away," Magnoli details. "Basically, I spent those eight days talking to Prince, Morris Day, Jerome Benton, and Vanity, and going to clubs."

Among the other talents Magnoli met were members of the Time like Jellybean Johnson, members of the Revolution Dr. Fink and Bobby Z, and of course, Wendy and Lisa, Prince's guitarists. It was their job not merely to answer Magnoli's questions but also—at Prince's urging—to take dancing lessons and go to acting school to prepare for the film.

"I literally stayed up for eight weeks and maybe got two hours' sleep a night, because I would work with the musicians whenever they woke up," Magnoli says. "Musicians don't wake up till around one in the afternoon. So at around one o'clock I'd be on their doorstep and ask them a ton of questions, and then I'd go from one to the other for the entire day."

One of the most popular aspects of *Purple Rain* remains, to this day, the comic relief, interplay, and light villainy of the Morris Day "dandy" character and his sidekick, Jerome. Magnoli was fascinated by this element of Prince's world.

"I had seen the interplay between Jerome and Morris Day, and I thought it would be a great counterpoint to Prince's iconoclasm: Prince's singularity as opposed to their orbit.

"[Morris and Jerome] are both calculating characters, but one does it with honey and one does it with a grenade. That was interesting drama there. So I got to meet Morris and Jerome during the eight weeks to research the film and their characters."

"It was such an innocent effort on everybody's part," Morris Day remembered of the efforts to make *Purple Rain*.

"Prince was like, 'We're going to make a movie,' and everybody was like, 'Okay.' He started lining up acting classes and dancing classes. . . . And I got kicked out of acting classes for always cutting up, just like my school days, when I'd get kicked out of class for the same kind of thing. And it turned out that that kind of cutting up is what worked for me in the film. So that was kind of my revenge on the acting teacher who kicked me out of class."[11]

Take Me with U: Selecting the Songs for *Purple Rain*

One of the most crucial aspects of preparing the *Purple Rain* script involved the selection of the music that would appear in the film, and ultimately on the soundtrack record. Albert Magnoli was invited by Prince to listen to one hundred un- released—but fully produced—songs and select a dozen for the project.

"He didn't come to me and say, 'I think you should choose number twenty-four because that's better than number eleven,'" relates the director. "He never said that. He just said, 'Okay, those are the songs? Okay.' He loved every one of them, but he loved them equally. He had written them in the moment and wasn't going to say that 'number ninety-six is more special to me than number ten, the one you selected.'"

To Magnoli's surprise, some of the great songs in that canon of one hundred prospective pieces still haven't been released, even to this day. This seems to support a popu- lar fan legend that there are thousands of great unreleased Prince songs out there in a vault somewhere.

One song, "Moonbeam Level," would be a crushing hit right now, according to Magnoli. "I was wishing I could have more music," he explains, "but I couldn't. Nobody was talking about a double album. No one ever suggested it."

Electric Intercourse: Changes from Script to Stage

William Blinn's script, originally titled *Dreams*, was later altered and rewritten substantially by Magnoli, essentially becoming a whole new movie in the process. Still, some elements were retained, particularly a humorous moment between Morris Day and Jerome Benton that harks back to comedians Abbott and Costello's most famous routine: "Who's on first?"

"The who's on first thing . . . that was the only thing from the William Blinn script that I pulled out," Magnoli says. "He had written it in a different way. I rewrote it to make it work for what I was doing with the characters at this point. But it was an idea that was originated with the William Blinn script."

By and large, the new Magnoli script told a different story about Prince: one less about the specter of death in general and more, unconventionally, about the individual demons (and cycle of domestic violence) torturing and influencing the young artist known as The Kid.

As for that memorable moniker, Magnoli noted, "I didn't want to call him Paul or Frank, or even Prince." In fact, Cavallo actually called Prince "The Kid," and Magnoli said, "Let's just go with what it's easy to call him."

Furthermore, there were dramatic changes between Magnoli's shooting script and the finished picture. In broad strokes, these changes involved the character envisioned for Vanity but eventually played by Apollonia.

In the Magnoli script, Vanity is far more hard-edged than, finally, Apollonia. In the famous Lake Minnetonka sequence, for instance, she is angrier over The Kid's practical joke lakeside, calling him a "bastard" and a "prick." These lines were dropped from Apollonia's character. Additionally, the original scene, as written, ends not with a romantic rapprochement between The Kid and his new girl, but with Vanity "cold" and "triumphant," hitching a ride with a pickup truck driver. The Kid is left in the dust, literally.

In other words, Vanity's scenes play as far more adversarial, whereas with Apollonia the sequence—particularly Prince's final rejoinder, "Don't get my [motorcycle] seat all wet"—plays as more romantic, and as playful, even harmless.

Another scene in the Magnoli script has Vanity attempting to ingratiate herself with a nonplussed club owner, Billy Sparks, but failing rather egregiously. She mentions her sick mother and doesn't seem to remember what city she's in. Between the lines, it's clear that Billy looks at her as grasping and a little desperate.

Later, following the explicit sex scene in The Kid's room, the script finds Vanity detecting a pretty serious scuffle between Prince's parents and leaving the house like a thief in the night. Immediately, she runs into Morris Day and Jerome Benton, and that's where their professional and personal seduction begins.

In the written version, The Kid takes some hard knocks too. Vanity's character informs him that "Morris Day is a better musician," a line ultimately dropped from *Purple Rain*. And furthermore, Morris tells Vanity (who knows better already) that The Kid isn't interested in "girls," a joke about Prince's sexuality that addressed, flat out, some fears about perceptions of his orientation. In the script, Vanity replies to Morris's put-down that she "knows" that The Kid isn't interested in girls; rather, he likes "women."

Another difference from script to shooting involves the controversial scene in which The Kid actually strikes Vanity/ Apollonia. In the script, he offers a more detailed apology for his bad behavior, saying that he just doesn't want Vanity "all around this stuff" regarding the musical world. He also asks her if she knows what "Morris is really all about."

Later in the script, Vanity responds aggressively to being struck, and confronts The Kid about his action. She tells him that he is "absolutely nothing" and has "spent" his entire life "hiding." Once more, these are moments that suit Vanity well, but seem not to fit the Apollonia character seen in the final film.

Morris Day and Jerome Benton also have more business in the screenplay than ended up in the final film. A running gag in the script involves Morris Day's caddy, and the perceived need for new hubcaps to tart it up.

Also, and perhaps most significantly, in the Magnoli script, The Kid's father succeeds in his suicide attempt, and The Kid does not dedicate a final song to his memory. Instead, The Kid merely (and rather undramatically) tells the audience, "I would like to do a song that two of my friends wrote," referring to Wendy and Lisa.

All Is [Not] Vanity, Sayeth the Lord

Once the script was satisfactory, however, an unexpected snag arose in preproduction. The beautiful Vanity (Denise Matthews)—a full-fledged member of Prince's entourage and also his girlfriend—had to make a difficult choice about starring in *Purple Rain*.

"At a crucial moment during the preproduction period, her agent had her meet Martin Scorsese," Magnoli remembers. Scorsese was prepping *The Last Temptation of Christ* (1988), and "he cast Vanity as Mary Magdalene.

"So she had a dilemma, because at the time, she was going to be gone when we were shooting *Purple Rain*,"

Magnoli recounts. "She came to me and said, 'What should I do?' And I replied, 'What would I do as an actress? *That would be simple*. I don't have to inflate what I'm doing here. Just be careful and make sure they're actually doing it. It's a controversial subject and you don't know that it will get budgeted.'

"Well, evidently she talked to Prince and they had it out, and he said, 'You should stay.' But she wanted to go out and forge her own destiny," Magnoli remembers. "She chose to go, which left us two weeks to find her replacement.

"We went everywhere, on a nationwide hunt," Magnoli said, remembering that between 500 and 1,000 girls were actually tested for the role of Prince's girlfriend. Legend even has it that an offer was put out to *Flashdance* star Jennifer Beals, who turned the role down.

"And literally, you know, Apollonia was the last person who walked into the room after two weeks of looking."

Apollonia, then known simply as Patricia Kotero, was a California-based actress of Mexican descent, and there was a powerful difference between her and all the Vanity wannabes who appeared at the auditions.

"What I liked about her immediately was that she didn't show up made up," Magnoli explains. "She got a call from her agent and came right over from the gym. She had on a gray T-shirt, a gray sweatshirt, and she had on baggy sweats. She didn't look glam at all, with her hair up in a ponytail. And she came in and she was just so sweet. And I said, 'There's something about this girl.' It was totally the opposite [of Vanity]. She's very soft.

"I called Prince and said, 'Find out if she can sing and if there's anything you can do with her.' He came over and picked her up, and they spent about three hours in the studio. He called me on the phone, and he said, 'Listen, if this is your choice, I can make it work. I can get music out of her.' And I said, 'Okay, do you want to do this?' And he said 'Yeah.' So I met Cavallo, and he met with her.

"She softened the movie a lot," Magnoli reflects. "I knew that was very good for me, just in terms of her natural beauty. I was concerned about the music, but they put together a pretty good song, and they had that one number ["Sex Shooter"]. They actually toured as Apollonia 6 for a time. They were successful musically on their own, under the tutelage of Prince.

"It would have been interesting with Vanity," Magnoli believes. "That would have been a wholly darker thing. Vanity just absorbed space in a different way than Apollonia. She's just a girl swept up by Prince and Morris Day.

"Vanity was very suspicious of everybody. She would have been looking at them both a little cockeyed. It would have created a lot of tension: a lot of good tension, a lot of dramatic tension. I'm happy with what Apollonia did, but there's no doubt you always wonder what Vanity would have done.

"There was also a natural evolution," Magnoli points out. "Vanity was leaving before I even arrived in Minneapolis to pitch to Prince. She already had a foot out the door. She was already on her way out. So I kind of inherited that situation. I knew it was fraught with a lot of tension. Scorsese's offer was just the icing on the cake. That was the impetus for her to make a decision. The unfortunate thing is that the Scorsese film was pushed back, and by then, she was out of contention. I met her a year later in a parking lot at MGM. She said, 'Man, did I make a mistake or what?' And I said, 'You can't think of it as a mistake, it's just what was.'"

Saturday Night Fever

The Magnoli script for *Purple Rain* was sent to film executives at Warner Bros. studio for approval, and hopefully a green light . . . and more funding.

Magnoli, as well as Cavallo, Fargnoli, and Ruffalo, went to Hollywood to make their case for the movie with the executives. Although Robert Cavallo does not specifically recall the following incident, he acknowledged that he had "some strange things happen" in his experience collaborating with the studio.

But Magnoli remembers a peculiar meeting in Hollywood during which a strange request was made.

"We think this is a pretty interesting project," Magnoli remembers an executive saying to him. "Would you mind John Travolta playing the role of Prince?"

The director's retort was simple. "'Gentlemen, we're making a film about someone who actually exists: Prince. This is his story,'" Magnoli relates. "'And the audience is going to be gunning for us, because unless it's an authentic story they're going to realize that Hollywood just mucked it up.'

"So I said, 'We need to stay authentic. The only thing we have going for us is authenticity. Prince is writing and performing the music, and that's it. Anything less than that and we don't have a movie, we just have a product no one is going to appreciate once the movie is done.'"

Then, Magnoli recalls, the details of the script came up, and the floodgates were opened.

"It's misogynistic," the studio complained, according to the director. Of particular concern was a scene in which a young woman, an acquaintance of Day, ended up thrown into a trash dumpster by Jerome.

Again, Magnoli saw the admittedly politically incorrect behavior as being authentic to a particular culture in which women were typically not treated very well. "I mean, the women are treated a little bit like plastic dolls," he notes. "So there was this misogynistic aspect to the material that they were very angry about. And they expressed their anger, and I said, 'I'm just revealing a culture. This is a culture. I'm not making this up. This is it. Anything less than that is a lie, so no, I'm not going to change that either.'"

Facing such requests to rewrite his script, Magnoli just wanted to return to work, to moviemaking in Minneapolis.

"*We should steer clear of these guys*," he remembers thinking about the studio bigwigs. "They were coming at me because they were saying, 'I can't get an audience in a room,' and 'This is scaring us.' 'This is a little too dark, a little too black, a little too urban. We're going to get slammed by the women's groups,' and on and on.

"And because no one had ever made a movie like *Purple Rain* before," Magnoli suggests, "this was all new territory. And there's nothing worse than a studio embarking on new territory. It's not in their DNA. People get fired when they try something new. They were not aware of Prince at all. They were just talking. They weren't aware of anything. *Anything*.

"From that meeting, we walked out of the room and Cavallo, Fargnoli, and Ruffalo were stunned," Magnoli recalls. "'We've got five more meetings like this!' Now that they had me in Hollywood, they wanted me to go to four more of these things, and I did. And after it was all over, with various degrees of insanity at each one, David Geffen's attitude was

Prince as Christopher Tracy in the box office flop *Under the Cherry Moon* (1986), which he also directed.

TOP: *Purple Rain* director Albert Magnoli sets up a shot on the set of *American Anthem* (1986).

BOTTOM: When Vanity dropped out of *Purple Rain*, Apollonia—Patricia Kotero—stepped in and rocketed to stardom.

Apollonia and The Kid fall in love in *Purple Rain*.

The Kid "goes crazy" at the First Avenue Club in *Purple Rain*.

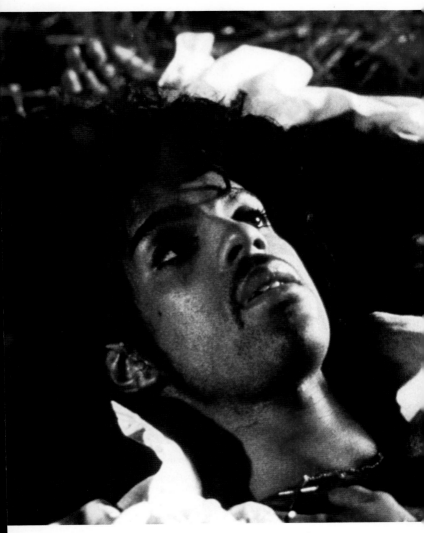

Darling Nikki? The Kid makes love with Apollonia in *Purple Rain*.

TOP: A muse (Ingrid Chavez) and The Kid parlay in the unofficial sequel to *Purple Rain*, called *Graffiti Bridge* (1990).

BOTTOM: In *Graffiti Bridge*, the dandy Morris Day and his sidekick Jerome Benton return to make trouble for The Kid, now a nightclub owner.

Morris Day and the Time take the stage in *Graffiti Bridge*.

The theatrical poster for *Purple Rain*.

that Prince would never sell movie tickets: 'It won't open.' Consequently, I learned reading his biography that he had already made a deal with Michael Jackson, so there was no way David Geffen was going to endorse a Prince movie after he had inked a deal with Jackson."

In fact, shortly after the release of *Purple Rain*, it was announced that Geffen and Jackson would be producing a major musical together within a year, and that the film would be a result of "a very special relationship David Geffen and Michael have enjoyed for many years."[12]

"Quite honestly, in real life, there was always artistic competitiveness [between Jackson and Prince], but they never had a harsh word to say about one another. *Ever*. Michael named one of his sons Prince. I don't know what that's about, and neither does Prince. But never did Prince say one word of negativity against Michael in my presence, and he had every opportunity to," Magnoli relates. "He grew up watching Michael Jackson, and he honored Michael Jackson."

Regardless of any perceived or real conflicts of interest at the studio, the biggest bone of contention among the suits involved a crucial element of the *Purple Rain* script: the suicide of Prince's abusive father. Cavallo also recalls that this was a big deal to the brass, and the studio didn't want the character to die. In part, this may have resulted from another Warner Bros. film, *Star 80*.

That effort, directed by Bob Fosse and released on November 10, 1983, featured a behind-the-scenes show-business aspect and also a suicide—like the prospective *Purple Rain*. And *Star 80*, about real-life tragic centerfold Dorothy Stratten, had not done well at the box office.

"They had already done their murder-suicide movie," says Magnoli, "and so they didn't want to come out with *Purple Rain*. It's not about the individual product, it's about the brand."

This final hurdle was almost insurmountable. Magnoli was asked to alter the script so that Prince's father would survive his suicide attempt. But Magnoli remembers that Cavallo didn't push him one way or another and was instead entirely supportive of his creative process and final decision.

"After these meetings, I couldn't wait to get back to Minneapolis," Magnoli recalls. He also remembers the words of the executives: "We're not saying no. We really want to explore this." Robert Cavallo told them "Okay," but also, according to Magnoli, that "Magnoli's going back to work."

At the final meeting to green-light or drop *Purple Rain*, Magnoli had to make a critical decision about the very direction of the film itself. Was he going to hang the entire film on one story element? Or was there another alternative? What would he lose? What would he gain?

"Terry Semel and Bob Daly were running the studio," Magnoli elaborates. "My meeting was with Terry Semel and Bob Daly, so I had to come in and do my dog-and-pony show. I started from the beginning of the movie and really did not know what my decision would be when I got to that point in the movie [regarding the suicide]. That's how I work sometimes. I let the organic quality of the story come out.

"It's a high-wire act. . . . In this case, I came right up to the moment. 'And then the father reaches to shoot himself, and Prince puts on the light, and he fires'—and then I paused and said to myself, *Does he die, or now what?*"

The answer came to him, and he went with it.

"'And then the police come. The father is alive on the cement floor. Prince watches as his father writhes in pain, and the police pull him out of the room. Prince is alone with the officers, who want to know what happened. . . .'

"At that moment, I realized, *I can get it all, even though he doesn't die, because the impact on Prince will be the same.*

"They were all relieved I didn't kill the father," Magnoli remembers. "That's probably what made them blossom the way they did. *We were in.* We were making this movie. They made the decision right on the spot. They hadn't even heard the music yet. But they knew my passion for the material. And Cavallo will tell you they're not stupid. They made sure they had a back-up [plan] by owning a percentage of the album. Their investment would be protected. If the film tanked, they could at least get some of their money back off the album."

Here, Magnoli paused to stress the importance of Cavallo, a man and colleague he considers a great producer and a steadfast ally. "He's in the room experiencing my passion, but he also has to stay later and talk the back-room crap. He smartly didn't tell me about things unless I needed to know them, unless it was something that had to come out of my mouth at a certain time. Those back rooms are nutty."

So Warner Bros. was happy with the final pitch and authorized *Purple Rain*'s budget, approximately $7 million. At long last, the movie was officially a go.

Come On In, the Water's Fine: Shooting at Lake Minnetonka

Purple Rain was slated to begin principal photography the first week of November, 1983, but everyone was actually ready the previous weekend, the last weekend in October. Director Magnoli did not want to get into dialogue and characterization yet, but the production had acquired the services of a helicopter for a day. Magnoli was thus able to block and shoot a major exterior sequence in the film, Prince and Apollonia's autumnal motorcycle drive to a rustic lake. It was a perfect day for shooting, with leaves falling and vivid colors on all the trees.

After the motorcycle ride was filmed, the shoot picked up from there the next week, with Apollonia's "initiation" by Prince, her infamous, topless jump into what she mistakenly believes is Lake Minnetonka.

Magnoli recounts, "I started on a Monday, and we're shooting Apollonia jumping into the water. Well, the difference between Friday and Monday was about forty degrees in the wrong direction."

Winter had arrived in Minneapolis. It was so cold, in fact, that some cast and crew members remember gasoline actually freezing in their cars.

"So Apollonia showed up on the set and it was literally hovering in the twenties and thirties, and there's a wind. *It's cold*," Magnolis stresses. "I show up at the set and the set nurse comes to me and she says, 'There's no way you're shooting Apollonia jumping in the water today.'"

Magnoli responded quizzically, "Why is that?"

The nurse replied, simply, that she'd die of shock.

Magnoli still remembers his impish response to the nurse, who was from Minneapolis and not an experienced Hollywood "movie" nurse. "They [the studio] will kill Apollonia before they tell me I can't shoot this scene,'" the director told her. "You can say what you want, but she's going into that water."

"The look on her face was just so sweet," he remembers.

Next it was time to convince the starlet that she was going swimming. After preparing the scene with safety divers in the water and a heated tent on the shore, Magnoli made his pitch. "I know the water is cold, and it may not be pleasant. We're going to have some divers under the water. Your job is just to jump in. Don't try to come out to shore. Let them grab you underwater and bring you right to shore," he instructed.

A trouper, Apollonia played the scene. She disrobed and enthusiastically leaped into the water.

And then immediately went into shock.

"She was in real trouble. Her body had shut down," Magnoli remembers. While she was nursed back to health, Magnoli had to consider his next move. He even tried to convince Apollonia to go back in the water to get the second shot of her leaving Lake Minnetonka, but it was definitely a no go this time. She'd had enough.

"'We have to shoot this somewhere else,' I said to Bob. 'I can't get her to come out [of the tent].' We were really screwed."

One day in, and *Purple Rain* was already behind schedule. Later, after shooting in Minneapolis was finished, Warner Bros. put up approximately half a million dollars to complete the Lake Minnetonka scene. Though it appears seamless onscreen, Apollonia's dip is pure movie magic.

"She jumped into a lake in Minneapolis and jumped out in Los Angeles," Magnoli recalls, laughing.

Purple Prose: Further Tales from the Shoot

Magnoli also remembers another funny story from early in the production schedule, involving the studio's general cluelessness about the Prince persona.

"The first day of shooting, Prince was in purple with the ruffled shirt and the buttoned pants, and he's standing in a farmyard in Minneapolis, and the studio head shows up and he goes, 'Why is he wearing that? I don't get it. Where are we in the script?'

"The question wasn't posed to me," Magnoli points out. "It was posed to the producer, Cavallo. He had to say something to the effect of, 'Well, he was at the nightclub performing the night before, and came out here.' And the studio head said, 'Okay.' But he was baffled by the outfit."

Again, this demonstrates that Prince wasn't so much an unproven commodity to Hollywood as an absolutely unknown one.

When the conversation turns to what it was like to direct Prince, Albert Magnoli remembers a sense of enjoyment and admiration. He also feels the actor was good at taking direction. "The relationship worked great," he affirms. "The interesting thing is that I never felt he couldn't take direction, because he's a musician. And based on my whole experience in that scene as a kid, it's an extremely disciplined world. If you're going to be successful, you have to be disciplined. And I already knew inherently that Prince was a clean liver. He didn't smoke and he didn't drink. He had an enormous work ethic and commitment to work, and made sure that the people around him felt the same way, or he got rid of them. So even if their prior history in the business was one of a haphazard approach to the whole thing, when they got involved with his organization, they basically realized, 'Okay, this is boot camp.'

"There was a wonderful camaraderie and wonderful work ethic in place already when I got there," he explains further. "So bringing the film business to them was just another kind of discipline. To be honest with you, the biggest hurdle was simply making them aware of the fact that we start shooting at seven a.m. That was the biggest thing they couldn't get. 'You start shooting *when*?' These kids were going to be falling asleep at seven a.m., not getting up."

One of the film's editors, Ken Robinson, also remembers the sense of discipline among Prince and his entourage. "Prince ran a very tight ship with the others in the cast. Not that Al wasn't in control on the set, but off, Prince was always making sure that people behaved."

The film was shot in forty days, with ten days devoted to musical performances at the schedule's end. "We did it film-school style," says Magnoli. "We did it raw, rugged, and ragged. We were making essentially a low-budget film for its time, with a very big reach, hopefully, because I wanted a crossover film."

However, sometimes during the shoot, Magnoli's steady pace and focus on "film-school style" stirred anxieties in Bob Cavallo, especially because he knew some important information that Magnoli didn't: *the movie was quickly running out of money*, and the production's bonding company was on the verge of taking the film out of Cavallo and Magnoli's hands.

Magnoli explains, "The bonding company is on the line for the budget, responsible for the bottom line."

Cavallo adds, "They were going to guarantee that it [the movie] had the proper standards for a proper film; that the proper technology was involved, etc."

"But it was constantly in my ear[, this voice] saying, 'You can't open the movie the way you did, it doesn't make sense. Start with the story, with Prince at home,'" Magnoli relates. "I said, 'Shut up, I'm not listening to you.'"

Although Cavallo personally liked the people at the bonding company and had a very good friendship with at least one of them, a fellow who had sponsored his admission into the Academy of Arts and Sciences, he remembers watching with a sense of dread as agents for the company pulled pages out of the script, folded them over, and instructed Magnoli to skip large swaths of the screenplay. "Oh, you can skip from here to here," they would say, according to Cavallo.

With the guarantors looking over their shoulders during the shoot, sometimes the pressure really built up.

"One night, he's doing a De Palma shot," Cavallo recalls of watching Magnoli in action, "and I said, 'What the hell are you doing? We gotta move on!' And it's Prince coming down a fire escape, and he's got the camera circling him. I said, 'You're gonna bankrupt me for a Brian De Palma shot!'

"It makes good filmmaking sometimes," Cavallo freely acknowledges, "but in the meantime, I had to shoot the story or we were going to go broke! The bonding company was going to take the film from us!"

Magnoli made a calculated decision to shoot the heavy dramatic scenes first and leave the musical numbers for last. This way, the actors would really get into character, almost without the distraction of their normal (musical) routine.

"I wasn't concerned about their discipline or passion to do it [the film]," Magnoli says. "That's half the battle.

And I figured that as long as I kept the environment comfortable and didn't distract them with all the filmmaking stuff at a hundred miles an hour and kept them in their safety zone—which is, 'I'm expressing words I would use in this situation myself'—they'd be okay. If you study the material, it is very straightforward but packed with emotion behind it, because every scene carries an emotional component.

"The telling moment for me in terms of Prince and his performance in the movie takes place in the dressing room. He's staring into the mirror and has the argument with Wendy and Lisa and the rest of the bandmates, and they storm out. And he's by himself with the little hand puppet and he's making that silly hand puppet sound, and then he starts listening to their music, and then the guy comes to the door and says, 'Hey, Kid, it's time to get onstage.'

"Those shots of Prince in the mirror, especially, to me concretize his character. You can see his emotional life. You can see his vulnerable life. You can see that he's pitted against his entire group, even though he's the leader of the group. And fortunately for me, I was able to get those scenes early. They helped define Prince for himself. He's got that scene of quiet alienation in the dressing room, and he's got the confrontation with the club owner, who's screaming at him, 'You're just like your old man!' and all that crap.

"Those scenes really defined Prince as an actor, as his character," Magnoli suggested. "They were really a lynchpin, and they were shot before I shot the scene of him with his father at the piano, where he talks about getting married. So that was important to me, because I knew that moment would be powerful."

That scene at the piano involved a highly experienced actor, Clarence Williams III of *The Mod Squad* (1968–1973) fame, and a relatively inexperienced one, Prince. "Going into a scene, you've got a nonactor and a very professional guy, but I wasn't concerned because I knew Prince had been prepared up to that moment," says Magnoli. "I knew that Prince would be completely stunned by the feeling in the room, despite the fact there was a film crew hanging around. We shot the dressing-room sequence first to let all those actors, all those performers, understand the emotions of the words, so the words would make sense."

"Clarence, to me, is a great actor. He's a studious guy and has great film weight. He's a charismatic guy. So when Prince walked in with Clarence . . . what Prince was feeling on his face, I can feel to this day. He's just one second from breaking out, and so is Clarence."

"Prince's inner life was very important, personally, to convey," Magnoli stresses.

Behind the Music: Shooting the *Purple Rain* Musical Performances

The musical performances had been saved for last during the making of the film, but this strategy presented a problem as the production fell behind schedule.

"We were three weeks behind when it came to shooting the music. It was near the end of the shoot," Bob Cavallo recalls. And the producer worried that shooting the musical sequences was going to be difficult. He consulted with Prince on the subject.

"'Albert's going to do thirty set-ups for every song,'" Cavallo remembers telling the artist. "He said, 'I'll give him one.' I said, 'Well, maybe two or three . . .'"

As it turned out, that wasn't the problem at all; rather, it was that Magnoli had originally desired to shoot the music sequences largely as he shot the rest of the film—shooting only what he needed (not necessarily for "coverage") for an edit that he had in his mind.

Magnoli explains further: "We hadn't spoken about this, but we were shooting the performances at the end of the movie and approaching it the same way we shot the movie. I knew what I needed and I set up cameras based on the edit, so I started doing that with the first song.

"And it threw Prince for a loop. And rightly so," Magnoli acknowledges. "Because now he's not into his performance.

He's only performing for the cut. It was my mistake. And Prince said, 'I can't do this, because I can't get into my performances.' Even though he was lip-synching, he was still singing, still performing. We didn't have live mics, so he's singing to his playback and his band was pounding their drums . . . we had no mics on them."

"I kept stopping. I stopped twice, and then Prince raised his hand and said, 'We have to talk, we have to work this out.' And I said, 'What's the problem?' He said, 'I can't get into my performance,' and I said, 'Okay.' We huddled, and I realized I needed to set up cameras, let him go from the beginning to the end of the song, call cut, and then set up cameras and go to the beginning of the song again."

There was just one problem.

"Well, that only gave me essentially four cameras per take. So that only gave me eight camera angles. Now, in a normal show, you'd have about twenty camera angles," Magnoli explains.

"So I said, 'Let's stop, I need to regroup. It's going to take about three hours. I need to get all four cameras on tracks— *dollies and tracks*—so I can move while the song is going on and not be restricted to four angles. I can have my cameras moving, and therefore harvest more angles while the performance is being undertaken.

"This is harder to do," the director readily admits. "So Prince went to relax and I had the crew build me tracks everywhere.

"So all four cameras are now on dollies and there are long tracks, 20 and 30 feet long, that allow me to go from the back of the venue to the front of the stage. And I have a parallel track going left to right, and then I put zooms on all the cameras, which the cinematographer never wanted to do, so I could constantly zoom and get closer and farther and wider, etc. I had to reinvent my approach in order to accommodate Prince's desire—rightly so—to really belt out the performance."

But this new approach would have a ripple effect on editing. Magnoli realized that suddenly he would have much more work to do in postproduction, because now he would have far more footage to sift through. He also realized that all the takes had to be watched carefully for continuity errors, since multiple takes would be compiled as a single performance in the final cut.

"I had my assistant and my script supervisor do it. Their whole job was to watch for wardrobe malfunctions," Magnoli describes. "I couldn't stop the take just because Prince's shirt unbuttoned, but then I had all this great footage that wouldn't match take one or take two. So I constantly had to analyze where I was."

There was another interesting complication. Amazingly, the concert-style footage shot at First Avenue Club (built originally as an art deco bus depot in the 1920s) was shot with something like 900 extras in attendance. It was, literally, a concert-sized crowd.

"They were all kids from high schools and colleges in the area," Magnoli explains. "They were being paid. We had put on our staff extra hair and makeup people, so they were being treated like stars. And the most interesting faces we pulled out for the glamour makeup. They all came prepared, and then we were able to get them processed in two to four hours. It was fantastic."

I asked Magnoli if he could explain the vibe among the audience there, watching Prince live, and he went into detail about the experience. "They were listening to the music. They came on the set at six a.m. and left at six p.m., but they spent the day watching Prince just inches away from them onstage, essentially performing. It was totally awesome, and—as anybody would be—they were fascinated by the filmmaking process. We kept them fed and hydrated, and they had to stand for a long time, but in between takes they'd drop to the floor and talk, and this was before cell phones and things that could distract them. And they formed this tribal community that lasted for seven to nine days."

In shooting the concert scenes with Prince and the Revolution, plus so many extras, Magnoli relied in part on his previous experience shooting musical performance sequences. "My thesis film at USC was called *Jazz*. There was a sequence set at a nightclub in Los Angeles, and we packed the place with people. And an interesting thing occurred when I was shooting. I noticed that when people clapped, their hands came into the frame. And I realized, based on the way that I lit the place, those hands were sort of glowing in the foreground of a lot of shots. It was just something that happened in my student film.

"And so when I came to this crowd, I framed the same way, knowing that the minute people started raising their hands, it would be another foreground object that would give me a visual story line that I didn't have to go around and cut to. You didn't have to cut to a person [enjoying the music] as long as you saw their hands in the frame. If you look closely, you'll see I utilize audience participation by using their hands.

"I spoke to Bob Fosse after the movie was made, and he commented on that," Magnoli remembers. "He asked me how I knew to frame that way, and I said, 'I learned it in film school.' He asked me how long it took to shoot, and I said, 'We did the whole thing in seven days.' And he said, 'That would have taken me seven months!' So many people have commented on it. So many people have been struck by it."

These shots not only provide a feeling for the venue and the specific audience but also capture what feels like a pre-existing, real-life moment. Magnoli had bartended through college, so he knew what he was trying for, and very well captured that moment: a live club, during a live performance, with waitresses holding trays in the air overhead while the audience jumped, danced, and swayed with the music.

"Another thing I duplicated was the movie *Woodstock* (1970)," Magnoli relates. "I love the way the announcer would announce the bands. 'Ladies and gentlemen . . . *Crosby, Stills, Nash*.' I loved the formality of the emcee announcing in essentially a prairie of hippies. The juxtaposition between that formality and the scene itself always intrigued me, so when we were making *Purple Rain*, I insisted on having the announcer. 'Ladies and gentlemen . . . the Revolution.' That's total homage to *Woodstock* and that announcer. I wanted that feeling because it set me up for an exciting experience. It had a big impact on me."

In staging the crowd/performance scenes of the film, Magnoli also looked back to another classic of the musical form, Bob Fosse's *Cabaret* (1972). "When Bob Fosse was so nice in his comments to me, concerning *Purple Rain*, I said, 'Listen . . . back at you.' I studied *Cabaret* so closely, and it was a big influence on me when I prepared for *Purple Rain*. When he packed the crowd in *Cabaret* . . . it was formal; mine was more jagged. I'm not dealing with Nazi Germany and the formality of the German culture; I'm dealing with kids, teen-agers, in their early twenties looking for escape. . . . There's more of a jagged feel to that. But the sense of it, the fullness of the frame was essential to me. That was all Bob Fosse."

This is actually an edifying comparison between produc-tions. In *Cabaret*, the larger context was deadly serious: the rise of Nazi Germany and totalitarianism, pre–World War II. *Purple Rain* is serious too, but the apocalypse in the mak-ing is more intimate and personal in nature: the domestic abuse in The Kid's family and the effect this violence and abuse have had on his music, and more than that, on his relationships with women.

Bob Cavallo remembers with glee "throwing extras in front of a dolly" during several Prince performances at First Avenue, and his joy at the quick pace of the sequences.

"We got caught up, and got the movie done," he notes with a well-deserved sense of satisfaction.

Diamonds and Pearls: Editing *Purple Rain*

During principal photography on *Purple Rain*, the process of editing was also undertaken in Minneapolis, inside a con-verted hotel room. There, assistant editor Ken Robinson and another editor shared a room and worked on the film from October to December 1983.

Magnoli, by and large, preferred to stay out of the editing room and keep his mind on the exigencies of the shoot; that was the manner in which he liked to work.

"I can't shoot and then walk into the editing room that night and work on footage," the director explains. "It is two separate worlds to me. Some directors can, but I don't. I know what I shot and I know the way it's going to be cut together, and if I walk into the room and someone's cut it together differently, I will stop everything and fix it. As opposed to doing that, I just don't walk into the room.

"For whatever reason—-and who the hell knows any of this—I can see a tremendous amount of visual information and not get cluttered by it," Magnoli explains about his approach to cutting. "I always had that editing thing. I edited for Jamie Foley. I edited my film *Jazz*, which went on to win the student Academy Award. Editing was always an essential lynchpin for me, so I don't get flustered by the process. I love the process. I actually get there as fast as I can, and I know what I need in order to get the cut that I need. So I wasn't overwhelmed by it."

The editorial assembly of the picture continued at the Sam Goldwyn facility off Fuller in Los Angeles until the following summer. When shooting was completed, Magnoli joined the party as the head editor in the process.

"I was an editing assistant and professor at USC when Al was there, and I advised him on his films as a mentor," Robinson explains. "Al offered me the job on the film since I had mentioned I was interested in cutting a feature. I had been teaching and cutting smaller films. Teaching takes up a lot of time."

Robinson remembered the process of editing the film and showing the dailies to the cast. "Prince was a remarkable person to work with. He saw his dailies and what needed to be improved, and [in] the very next set of dailies, you could see that improvement. However, he demanded the same of all the others as well."

One early scene proved difficult, per Robinson's memory: the sex scene in the barn (seen in a montage, late in the film). "That was done [during] the first days [of shooting] before they [Prince and Apollonia] got to know each other, and in some of the close-ups of Prince I could see his discomfort being shot with a naked woman sitting on him with all the crew around. Her footage was pretty straightforward in that scene. But it eventually worked."

And "the better he [Prince] got to know Apollonia, the better their onscreen relationship improved in the material,"

Robinson explains. "Because he knew everyone else, those relationships and that familiarity showed onscreen."

I asked Robinson if it was more difficult cutting a film in which the central performers were inexperienced actors, and he said that this was not the case. "You just look for the best performances and try to be [as] consistent as you can with their performances. They essentially were themselves, or close enough to it. Cutting Morris and Jerome was very easy, and in a way the first cuts emphasized them at the expense of Prince's character and story line; there was an imbalance of the two story lines."

Also per Robinson's memory, the film generally came together well. "Al had a very tight film in mind from the beginning. One of the requirements for the music numbers was that it had to look as though there were no edits, almost live. As an editor should, he [Magnoli] set the tone overall again for the music numbers."

In terms of narrative, "there was more give and take" than in the musical sequences, according to the editor. "There were many issues of story and characters needing clarification or balance."

An instance of this occurred when Prince dedicated the song "Purple Rain" to his father during the film's valedictory moment. In the original cut, The Kid simply noted that the song had been written by Wendy, but according to Robinson, there was no larger "meaning to that in the overall film." He agreed that dedicating the song to Prince's father "had more story value."

"That breakthrough moment was given to me by someone at Warner Bros.," Magnoli acknowledges. "And I realized that it would work whether the father died or lived, that Prince would dedicate that song, 'Purple Rain,' to his father. That line wasn't in it before. It was simply, 'I'm going to do a song written by Lisa and Wendy.' If you look at the movie, fortunately, the way I shot Prince, his lips were behind the microphone, and I was able to drop in the line about his father. That wasn't scripted. That came later."

In terms of narrative flow, there was never any debate about beginning with "Let's Go Crazy" and the exciting montage. "Al wanted to show as much as he could and get the feeling of being there and participating," Robinson explains. The opening, in Robinson's words, grew "tighter and tighter" until it reached the urgent, brilliant final shape as seen in the film.

"Here's the interesting thing about that happening," Magnoli says. "I think it's seven minutes and change. It's totally unconventional. I wrote the script that way. I wrote the script and then discovered that 'Let's Go Crazy' was actually shorter than I needed. I needed seven minutes and the original was four and change, so Prince had to create, based on the script, an entire middle to that song that then became the song. "

As far as footage lost or deleted in the process of getting a final cut, most of it, according to Robinson, involved the "Morris and Jerome interaction. It was almost a feature and story in itself."

The Number One That Almost Wasn't: "When Doves Cry"

Interestingly, *Purple Rain*'s first hit single, "When Doves Cry," also emerged from the film's editing process.

Albert Magnoli explains: "It was written as I was editing the movie. I realized there was an opportunity for a song. I needed to get Prince from one place to another. It wasn't scripted there would be a song there, but as I was cutting, I realized I needed a song.

"So I went to Prince and told him what I needed, and he wrote—in twenty-four hours—'When Doves Cry.' I said, 'The subject matter would be you in relation to your mother and father and your relationship, ultimately, with Apollonia.'

"On the very next day, around noon, he called and said, 'I have a song.'"

In fact, Prince had written two. One was slower paced and one was fast paced. Prince asked Magnoli to come over to his studio (Sunset Sound Studio in Los Angeles) and listen to both so he could make a judgment.

"I went and I listened to the two songs," Magnoli remembers. "But I said, 'Let's go with "When Doves Cry."' I was happy the minute I heard it. This was going to work well for our needs. I was thinking about the rawness of it, the primal aspect of it. I was thinking of the archetypical aspects and the urgency of it, and what it would do for this section of the film."

"So Prince said, 'Great,' and gave me some kind of cassette, I guess it was, in those days. I then went back to the studio and had the cassette put onto film, and now had it in the editing room to begin cutting the footage to the music."

The only problem: some folks who also listened to "When Doves Cry" insisted that it wasn't actually finished at all. They felt it needed something more.

For one thing, the new song lacked a traditional bass guitar line. Prince did not include one, because he felt that it made the song sound too conventional.[13]

When Magnoli was confronted about this so-called "missing" element in "When Doves Cry," he thought the controversy was absurd. "I said, 'It's good enough for me. I think it's great. If Prince decides to add more instruments to it, it won't change my synch, so I can continue my work, but I think we're fine.'"

But Prince was still being hectored by some advisors in his inner circle about the song. The artist called up Magnoli.

"So let me ask you something, do you think this song is done? Because they're telling me to add more instruments."

Magnoli's only response was that the song was "stripped down" and "great."

"One thing about Prince," Magnoli explains, "when he gets the urge to do music and then is done . . . *he's done*. He doesn't want to rethink it. He doesn't want to add the frills. He's like me. When he's done, he's done.

"The fascinating thing about all of this is how it starts out with an artistic need," Magnoli muses. "The need is fulfilled by an artist such a Prince, who can do it very quickly. Then the bureaucracy kind of surrounds you. They come at me. They come at him. Certain people are like little visionaries and say, 'It's not done. It's really not done,' hoping that one of us cracks and says, 'It really isn't done,' and one of us should be paranoid about this."

Ultimately, nobody cracked. No musical additions or alterations were made to "When Doves Cry" . . . and it promptly became the first number one hit from the *Purple Rain* soundtrack.

"It was an instant sensation," reports Magnoli. "That's the irony of all this. That's the one that Prince said should be the first one, and of course, everybody disagreed."

"When Doves Cry" works in the film as a perfect marriage of visual and audio. "It says where Prince is, what the

problem is, and [that he] has the open road before him,"
Magnoli says. But because the song was actually released
before the movie, Magnoli wonders if perhaps "When
Doves Cry" gives away too much of the film's central conflict (Prince's shabby treatment of women and the way he
relates that to his negative experience with his abusive father
and abused mother).

"The lyrics were right on. They actually told a crucial
part of the movie prior to the movie being seen by people,
which had to do with the father and mother," the director
considers. "So when Apollonia comes through the back yard
with Prince and sees the mother and father [and asks about
them], well, the audience already knew it was his mother and
father. So had I recognized earlier the power of the song, I
probably could have taken that [exchange] away and just
had her look at them. It's funny how you have to be aware
of these things. And if you're not . . . you're going to learn."

Also, it was interesting that Prince could have lifted the
montage right out of the film, intact, and had a ready-made
video for "When Doves Cry," edited by his movie director.
Yet he opted instead to do something original, a less overtly
visual, more intimate thing, a kind of tangent based on the
film.

"The video of 'When Doves Cry' had Prince in a tub
or something," Magnoli recalled. "There's a picture of his

mother on the bureau, and he's looking at the mother. And he's using some footage of the cast running around. It's related somehow. But it was just him doing something: having a day at home by himself and thinking it through, to the picture of his mother. And he used a picture frame from the movie and put his mother in it."

And of course, the video turned out to be a big hit too.

Let's Go Crazy: Testing *Purple Rain*

With the film mostly edited, save for the musical sequences (which appeared almost as live in this early cut), Cavallo and Magnoli screened the rough cut of the film for Warner Bros.

"I made sure that the film they saw was a real picture," Magnoli says. "As soon as they saw the first cut, they came back and said, 'What do we need to do to help you finish this? This is amazing.' They were totally on board, and I said, 'Get rid of the bonding company because they're bugging me.'"

Cavallo needed something else to finish the movie: *cash*. In particular, the production required approximately half a million dollars to polish the film and finish a second period of shooting in Los Angeles (namely the completion of the Lake Minnetonka sequence, where Apollonia had to exit the lake).

Michael Ovitz pressured Warner Bros. to give the movie six hundred grand by, in Cavallo's memory, "threatening to take the film elsewhere." This tactic is part of the reason Cavallo still has such fond feelings for him. Ovitz secured the money and Terry Semel demanded that the movie get "enough play dates to make the movie significant."

Still, this doesn't mean it was all smooth sailing.

On the horizon, another rock 'n' roll backstage musical was shaping up as competition for *Purple Rain*: *Hard to Hold* (1984), starring musician Rick Springfield. The film featured Springfield as Jamie Roberts, a famous rock star romancing a child counselor played by Janet Eilbert.

Yet where *Purple Rain* retained its rough edges and sense of authenticity, director Larry Peerce's effort played as an unrealistic, silly, ultimately inconsequential farce. In particular, the climactic set piece of the film was a "sold-out" concert, but Jamie just played one song there and left, hoping to resolve his romantic crisis with Eilbert. In my *Rock and Roll Film Encyclopedia* of 2007 (Applause Books), I called *Hard to Hold* "Hard to Stomach."

"Interestingly enough, when I completed *Purple Rain*, people were concerned because *Hard to Hold* was coming out at the same time," Magnoli remembers. "The studio was nervous and said, 'Al, you have to check this movie out.' So I saw the movie and I said, 'Just keep on the track we're on. Don't even think about it.' He [Rick Springfield] got caught in the Hollywood shuffle. He listened to whoever was the genius in the studio, and they compromised the crap out of it. As a result, we had no problems."

After all the editing on *Purple Rain* was complete and the studio had screened the finished picture, it was time to preview it for an audience. Cavallo remembered that first test screening with enthusiasm.

"It was down at the MGM Theater in Culver City, and Terry Semel got furious with me. The numbers were so high that he thought we had engineered to have Prince's fan club in the audience. So he said, 'We're going to do another screening, and for the next one, you won't know where it's going to be until you're on the Warner Bros. jet!' I said, 'Terry, do you think I'm an idiot?' Like this [studio] is some radio station we're going to screw around with?!"

"It was screened for an all-white audience," Magnoli recalls, "but the appreciation numbers went through the roof. So next they take us to Texas, to a redneck crowd.

"Well, we play the movie and it goes through the roof again," Magnoli says. "Now they know they've got something."

Which didn't mean the studio wasn't still a bit twitchy about *Purple Rain*. In particular, they had a problem with the scene in which a female talent (and former girlfriend of Morris Day) unceremoniously ends up in a dumpster.

"They said, 'We saw the cut and we're thinking that may be a little rough,'" the director relates. Magnoli's take was that the suits should just wait to see how it played with the screening audiences and then make a final decision whether or not to include it.

"Of course, it played great," he explains. "They [the audience] were standing on their feet, roaring in laughter."

But even after that affirmation, the studio still wasn't so sure, and so removed the scene for the follow-up preview. There, the moment in the film was greeted with dead silence.

"If you take it out, there's nothing in that moment," Magnoli reflects. "Accordingly, the studio executives came back and said, in all earnestness, 'We like it the way with the dumpster!' contradicting everything they said in previous meetings."

Even this was not the end of the crazy back-room meetings.

"Now we've screened it for two major white audiences, in two different major demographics, high end and redneck," Albert Magnoli explained. "The movie is done, it's locked. It's ready to be marketed. Then we have a meeting with the geniuses in marketing in Warners. These guys come in . . . and their suits are beautiful. They come in and sit down, facing me and Cavallo, and one of the geniuses says right off the bat, 'Understand, Al, you've essentially made an urban movie that will play for one weekend to fourteen-year-old-and-under black girls, period.'

"That was his statement, in spite of the fact that we had just had two screenings in front of white audiences."

Magnoli was incensed by the suggestion that *Purple Rain* was nothing but a niche film, and asked one of the marketers, "What do you do? Where do you get this information? Can you show me the information?"

When access was refused, Magnoli answered the charge that *Purple Rain* was a niche film with a market analysis of his own making. "I'll tell you what. Do I look like a black fourteen-year-old urban girl? I made this movie for forty-five-year-old white women who think that Prince is sexy, period. It's gonna go crossover immediately, based on what you already know," he said.

"The music spoke to everybody it needed to speak to."

A Star Is Born

Purple Rain opened in 900 theaters nationwide on July 27, 1984. The red carpet movie premiere at Mann's Chinese Theater was a major pop culture coming out for Prince, hosting celebrities, rock stars, and movie icons the likes of Steven Spielberg, Eddie Murphy, and even the members of Fleetwood Mac. MTV hosted a premiere party TV special for *Purple Rain*'s big day that has since become the stuff of legend.

When the first box office numbers were tallied in late July, it was clear that *Purple Rain* was also destined for box office gold. The film opened in the number one slot and made back its budget and more—$7.75 million—its first weekend.

Even more impressively, the backstage musical knocked the sci-fi comedy blockbuster *Ghostbusters*—the number one film of the summer—from its top perch. Although this was quite an achievement, director Magnoli remembered being rather nonplussed by the whole "battle" with the Bill Murray supernatural comedy.

"I thought two things," he elaborated. "I thought we'd won a round—not that I was even engaged in a battle. But I also knew that *Ghostbusters* was made for a specific reason, and it was made very broad, and that whatever we were able to harvest for one weekend would pale in comparison to what *Ghostbusters* would do as a franchise.

"So to me it was *Okay, fine, great*," he continues. "It confirmed to me what I had known, that we had a crossover film, and we'd not compromised it by going Hollywood . . . otherwise we wouldn't even be in the theaters anymore. It was just part of the mystery of this thing called Hollywood marketing. I thought, *Okay, great*, but I was already moving on. Once the movie is made . . . I don't have any regrets. Once

I give it my all . . . I am not concerned with what people do with the movie after that."

What remains remarkable about *Purple Rain* was that it had enough "legs" to play strongly not just for one weekend but all summer following its release.

"I credit a lot of the success of *Purple Rain* to Bob Cavallo, because he has a very astute sense of music, and as you know, he runs Disney now. He's a great guy," Magnoli says. "The thing about him is that he knew innately that he needed to follow 'When Doves Cry' with another song to keep *Purple Rain* in the movie theaters, and made sure another song was released. And then another single after that to make sure that the album as well as the movie would be served by the release of the record. Believe me: if Cavallo wasn't orchestrating it, the record companies weren't capable of doing it.

"The coordination of it was quite good. In these days, it seems almost revolutionary," said Magnoli. "Cavallo knew innately that once that film was made, what he had to do marketingwise was make sure the record would come off those racks."

"Terry Semel made sure that the movie kept playing," Cavallo notes with appreciation. "We did a lot of things you would do with a record. We had 'When Doves Cry' and 'Let's Go Crazy' well in advance of the film. Then we had 'Purple Rain.'"

Cavallo is also quick to credit two other talents as well. "It's a good film. Magnoli did a great job. We had $70 million the first year; and that would be well over $200 million today."

The other talent he highlights is the film's star, Prince. "I thought Prince was a genius. He could do anything he set his mind to, including act. He was fantastic [in the movie]."

Ultimately, the film and album generated two number one hits, which is an extraordinary achievement. Even more extraordinarily, the album sold some 205,000 copies just on *Purple Rain*'s opening day.[14] Some 13 million copies of the album sold, and *Purple Rain* even knocked Bruce Springsteen's album *Born in the U.S.A.* from the top *Billboard* slot for a whopping 24 weeks.

Prince himself scored a new record with *Purple Rain*. For a time in the summer of 1984, he boasted the top song, the top album, and the top movie in the country, a troika not achieved since the heyday of the Beatles in the 1960s.

"I think we expected a great response," says film editor Ken Robinson, "but no, I think most were surprised" that the film garnered such popular acclaim.

The film also achieved unexpected success with the critical establishment. The two most influential film critics of the day, Roger Ebert and Gene Siskel, not only gave the backstage musical "two thumbs up" on their program *At the Movies*, they both put it on their top-ten best of the year list, a fact that director Magnoli was not even aware of until this reporter informed him of it.

Other critics were equally enthusiastic. *Films in Review*'s John Nangle called *Purple Rain* "easily the best of the MTV-influenced rock-video-styled movies" and noted that it "explodes with grand opera passions and imagery that compensate for its fragmented storyline and leave us breathless victims of an artist who connects with an audience mood and never lets up."[15]

Meanwhile, the *Los Angeles Times*'s Sheila Benson noted that the film is "hot, jagged," and "garish," and that it "succeeds beyond even its own audacious dreams."[16]

The plaudits were so strong that *Purple Rain* was even described as "the generational breakthrough of *A Hard Day's Night*."[17] Many critics even compared the film to *Citizen Kane* (1941), widely held to be the greatest film of all time.

That latter bit of praise was just too much for the modest Magnoli. "Okay, that's great," he says off-handedly. "You can't get too crazy about it. I understand what he [the critic] said, but I go back filmically to *Citizen Kane*'s use of camera, use of long lens, use of black-and-white, and use of the studio crane.

"I had the opportunity to literally listen to the footage of *Citizen Kane*, prior to them redoing the footage, and you can literally hear the dolly—those massive dollies they used at the time—creaking over the wooden floors of the studio. And of course, he's doing these elaborate dollies, which nobody ever did, with equipment we consider antiquated. I take it with a grain of salt, because I know what Orson Welles was doing at the time: he was completely exploding film expression with equipment that was based on essentially setting up a proscenium arch and shooting the hell out of it, but not really moving the cameras. Then Orson Welles shows up and starts moving the camera and says, 'I want this crane to go from here to there,' and everyone else says, 'Are you fucking kidding me?'"

Yet the hyperbole is understandable in at least one sense. *Citizen Kane* revolutionized "film language," and to a large extent, *Purple Rain* undeniably did the same thing, at least as far as how music is visualized in modern, post-MTV film, particularly in terms of those brief montages called "videos." The incorporation of these vignettes into a narrative was a very big deal in the early years of MTV. *Purple Rain* essentially used video montages to convey by shorthand a remarkable amount of important narrative and character information.

"I had an MTV film executive come to me at the premiere of *Purple Rain*," Magnoli recalls. "He said, 'I'd like a statement from you about how MTV shaped your vision on *Purple*

Rain.' I said, 'I hate to inform you, but I don't even own a television. I never saw MTV.' He looked at me, shocked, and said, 'What do you mean you don't have a TV?' 'Well, I grew up in a household where my TV broke when I was five. I didn't have one when I was in college, I didn't have one in my apartment at USC, so I've never seen MTV.' He was completely flummoxed."

The success of *Purple Rain* also spawned a new and unexpected trend in eighties fashion, with the young adult crowd seeking to imitate Prince's flamboyant, almost anachronistic style. Fashionistas at the time noted enthusiastically that *Purple Rain* "has added romance to his [Prince's] raunch and inspired a whole new camp of followers. In downtown clubs and uptown boutiques, a princely look is emerging that's glitzy, irreverent and just the slightest bit in bad taste."[18]

In other words, *Purple Rain* wasn't just a hit of the summer of 1984. It was the pop culture event of the year.

The thrill of the *Purple Rain* experience also came back and hit Minneapolis hard. The town became "at least in the world's imagination," according to writer Rob Nelson, "the Caligula and ancient Rome of a brave new pop world."[19]

"I wasn't unaware of it, but the interesting thing is what occurred after the film hit the theaters. People flocked to

Minneapolis," Magnoli recalls. "They went to that club. I remember reading an interview with the owner of the bar, who said, 'This *Purple Rain* crap has made my business great, but it's also a fucking pain in the ass,' because people showed up thinking the bar is going to be the movie. But what we did in the movie is *the movie vision* of the bar. It was my vision from being a bartender in the past, to get saturated with visuals and a style, so we turned that space into what was turning me on. It was reality, but a heightened reality. So the owner was complaining, 'They're coming here expecting the scene.'"

The only sour note struck during the summer of 1984 came from some critics who viewed the Magnoli, Cavallo, and Prince film as decidedly antiwoman. In particular, *Newsday*'s Wayne Robins complained of *Purple Rain*'s "rampant misogyny" and wrote that the film's antiwoman attitude "undercuts some of the most viscerally moving rock concert footage ever presented in a motion picture."[20]

Robins was not alone in his perspective on the film and Prince's "scene." In *Texas Monthly*, critic James Wolcott wrote that "women in *Purple Rain* aren't allowed to be upright and sensible—they're in attendance upon His Moody Genius, who lords about as a priapic god and (I kid you not), prefers to converse with his hand puppet. Masturbation has always been a major theme in Prince's work, and it's easy to see why. Who needs a partner when you are your own greatest thrill?"[21]

Eventually, the Purple One himself was forced to address the whispers (and shouts) of the movie's misogyny. "Now, wait, wait. I didn't write *Purple Rain*. Someone else did. And it was a story, a fictional story, and should be perceived that way," he stated in an interview. "Violence is something that happens in everyday life, and we were only telling a story. I wish it was looked at that way, because I don't think anything we did was unnecessary. Sometimes, for the sake of humor, we may have gone overboard. And if that was the case, then I'm sorry, but it was not the intention."[22]

Critic David Denby seemed to accurately get the idea that underneath *Purple Rain* was a movie *about* misogyny in the culture (and overcoming it); the film was not actually misogynistic in nature. That was a distinction many simply did not understand, but Denby trenchantly noted that the issue of how women are treated by The Kid "is resolved when Prince sings 'Purple Rain,' a song written by two female members of the band that he had earlier scoffed at. The number, a long, solemnly ecstatic supplication with a healing gospel sound to it, is both an apology to women and a promise of erotic good times."[23]

Some (female) scholars went even further in defense of the film, suggesting that the jokes about Wendy's periods (that God has reversed them, making her act nice only one weekend a month) were deliberately undercut and subverted by that memorable final song, "Purple Rain."

"The song celebrates women," suggested the authors of *The Curse: A Cultural History of Menstruation.* "Women run, bathe and laugh in purple rain. Repeated again and again, the changed words 'purple rain, purple rain' echo the repetitious nature of the menstrual cycle. . . . Prince/Wendy invokes in 'Purple Rain' a menstrual celebration experienced vicariously through the woman participating in the ritual of wetness. In this miraculous lyric, at least, the goddess seems to have gotten Prince's period reversed."[24]

Such controversy aside, *Purple Rain* was undeniably an artistic and commercial triumph, and those involved in its production remember it that way to this day. "It was overwhelming as far as the nationwide recognition," Morris Day told *Essence* Magazine. "Minneapolis folks were treating us differently. Before we'd have to pay to get in a club and buy drinks, and finally when we could afford it, we were getting everything for free. It was all interesting because when we were struggling and could have used the help, we didn't get it."[25]

"I like the fact that in the film we were separate to his craziness . . . which we were," Wendy Melvoin notes of her participation as costar. "But at the end of the film, where he plays 'our' song, 'Purple Rain'—we didn't have that kind of glory in real life."[26]

Before the Year of *Purple Rain* was over, Prince picked up a well-deserved Academy Award for Best Original Song Score, as well as a Grammy for Best Album of Original Score Written for a Motion Picture or Television Special. Before awards season was done, "When Doves Cry" was also nominated for a Golden Globe Award for Best Original Song. In 2004, Prince and the Revolution won a "special" World Soundtrack Award on the twentieth anniversary of their "legendary" *Purple Rain*.

And if things had been just a little different, the world would have seen a follow-up to *Purple Rain* in theaters by the end of the 1980s. Robert Cavallo had a plan and a kernel of an idea . . . but Prince didn't bite.

"It was called *Purple Rain 2*," said the producer. "The Further Adventures of Morris Day and Jerome." In particular, the producer wanted to see the duo in Las Vegas, running afoul of the mob.

Finally, director Albert Magnoli got the last word regarding the making of *Purple Rain*: "We were fortunate that

Prince and I had a great, solid alliance, and I had a great alliance with Bob Cavallo."

"If You Start from *Citizen Kane*, Where Do You Go from There?" Prince on Film After *Purple Rain*

Following the unexpected success of *Purple Rain*, Prince could pretty much write his ticket in Hollywood. While Albert Magnoli went on to direct *American Anthem* (1986), a film about the professional rise of an American gymnast played by Mitch Gaylord, Prince inaugurated the *Purple Rain* tour in November 1984; it had 100 dates in the United States and sold an impressive 1.5 million tickets.

Afterward, the artist began to develop a follow-up film project called *Under the Cherry Moon* (1986), again with the team of Cavallo, Ruffalo, and Fargnoli.

Meanwhile, in an unexpected controversy, some American politicians retroactively targeted *Purple Rain* as a bad influence on children. Approximately a year after the film's release, *Purple Rain*'s overt sexuality became a bone of contention, particularly for Tipper Gore, then-wife of Senator (and later Vice President) Albert Gore.

One day, she apparently discovered her daughter Karenna listening to the Prince *Purple Rain* album, particularly the

searing and dramatic song "Darling Nikki," and was intense-
ly disturbed by the song's mention of masturbation, not to
mention pervasive talk of "sex fiends."

Allied with Susan Baker, wife of then Treasury Secretary
James Baker, Mrs. Gore promptly formed the Parents Music
Resources Center (PMRC) in May 1985. Its mission was to pressure record companies to "warn" parents of explicit sexual or
violent content through the use of a label notification program.

That label, reading "Explicit Lyrics—Parental Advisory,"
struck some as being both censorious and unnecessary, but
the Recording Industry Association of America nonetheless went along with Ms. Gore's moral crusade. However,
by 1989—some four years after the "Darling Nikki" incident
and the formation of the PMRC—"less than 4 percent of
albums released" bore "the advisory label."[27] In other words,
the controversy made a mountain out of a molehill.

Considering the incident and its impact nationally on
the music industry, it seems doubtful that Mrs. Gore ever
saw *Purple Rain* in the first place, or realized that the song
"Darling Nikki" was both designed and executed as a bad-
taste frontal assault, an attack, and was used in that way for
dramatic purposes.

Then again, context may not have mattered much, especially since Prince was becoming widely recognized as "the
pied piper for [a] sexually obsessed, sentimental and perhaps

classic generation of Americans who can relate to the beat of his histrionic musical configuration,"[28] at least according to Dr. Alvin F. Pouissaint in "An Analytical Look at Prince," which appeared in *Ebony* at roughly the same time that Ms. Gore began her censorship crusade.

Indeed, this is why the late film critic Pauline Kael approved, at least somewhat, of Prince and *Purple Rain*. She famously described him as "The fulfillment of everything people like Jerry Falwell say rock 'n' roll will do to the youth of America."[29]

While Washington, D.C. hotly debated sexually explicit lyrics and masturbation, Prince nabbed his first credit as a film director when the original helmer of *Under the Cherry Moon*, Mary Lambert (who later directed *Pet Sematary*), departed over creative differences. The film itself, though high-intentioned, turned out to be the proverbial "sophomore slump" for the popular musical artist.

Although the intent was to make *Under the Cherry Moon* resemble the light and breezy Fred Astaire musicals of the 1930s like *Swing Time* and *Top Hat*, the film—which starred Prince as a gigolo named Christopher Tracy frolicking in the south of France—lacked the requisite light touch, and played instead like something of a colossal ego trip.

In its ninety-eight excruciating minutes, *Under the Cherry Moon* (Warner Bros.) veered from bad camp to ridiculous faux tragedy. The movie ended with Christopher Tracy dead, as an angel singing love songs from a cloud on high. The tunes in the film were actually pretty good, included "Christopher Tracy's Parade," "Sometimes It Snows in April," "Kiss," and "New Position," but even some great Prince music couldn't rescue the terrible, misconceived film.

Predictably, all of Hollywood rose up like a tidal wave to attack the second Prince film, marking the beginning of a backlash that, in some circles, continues to this day. Critical reviews were negative, and audiences stayed away. The film opened in 941 auditoriums nationwide, a few more than *Purple Rain*, but did less business than its auspicious predecessor.

Writing for *The Charlotte Observer*, critic Joann Rhetts observed the crucial difference between the two Prince films:

"Besides the powerful soundtrack, *Purple Rain* had an actual story and a painful point to make about the loneliness of the long-distance rocker. *Under the Cherry Moon*, however, is as bleached of color and energy as the anemic black and white cinematography. It is an exercise in vanity, and we're not talking one of Prince's ladies in undies. We're talking an adolescent watching his face in the mirror, smooching the glass and imagining the girl of his dreams swooning beneath his lips."[30]

Under the Cherry Moon was made for almost twice the budget of *Purple Rain*, but did not earn its cost back. *Under the Cherry Moon* also "won" a record five "Razzie" (Golden Raspberry) awards, for Worst Picture, Worst Director (Prince), Worst Actor (Prince), Worst Supporting Actor (Jerome Benton), and Worst Song ("Love or Money"). The film was nominated for additional Razzies, including Worst New Star (Kristin Scott Thomas) and Worst Screenplay.

1986 was really proving a down year for Prince. In addition to the failure of the film, the year saw the disbanding of the Revolution, the band highlighted so lovingly in *Purple Rain*.

Soon, however, Prince had another reversal of fortune, starring in a terrific concert film made in Rotterdam, Holland, called *Sign 'o' the Times* (1987), produced by the troika of Cavallo, Fargnoli, and Ruffalo.

The concert film was shot during the Purple One's European tour and featured amazing music, some great stage effects (including mist, glowing electronic spheres, and blue neon light), and most importantly, high-energy performances from Prince, Sheila E., and Sheena Easton.

Albert Magnoli also worked on the film, in an uncredited capacity as director. "I was in Los Angeles developing another project, and Warner Bros. was looking for me to do another project with Prince, another musical. They were thinking they would do *Purple Rain 2*, and I said, 'I have something much better than that.'

"Prince at the time was in Europe, on tour with *Sign 'o' the Times*, so I said to Warner Bros. and Bob Cavallo, 'Send me to Europe, let me talk to Prince, let me sit down with him, hear this concert, and get some ideas.' This was 1986. I saw Prince, we hugged, and he asked me if I was going to stay around, and I said, 'For a few days.' I was going to try to figure out what we would do next. He said, 'Great.'

"When I saw the concert, I already knew what we were going to do next," Magnoli explains. "I wanted to do a musical called *The Dawn*. This was something we had talked about earlier, but listening to that concert, I just got inspired and said, 'Okay.' When Prince got off the stage, I said 'We're doing *The Dawn* next.'"

Unbeknownst to Magnoli, this idea of a new movie musical thrilled Prince to such a degree that he wanted to start immediately. "Cavallo called me and said, 'Prince is so excited, he doesn't want to tour anymore.' I said, 'He should stay on tour, because it's going to take me at least six or seven months to get this organized.'"

Nonetheless, Prince returned to Minneapolis, and the managers were left to deal with the financial fallout of the tour's unexpected end. Inventively, they came up with the idea of a documentary concerning the tour.

"They started shooting, and Cavallo said, 'Come and help us,' Magnoli recalls. "I went there and got the film shot and edited, and then went back to developing *The Dawn* film."

Unfortunately, that film was never made, but *Sign 'o' the Times* remains a great companion piece to *Purple Rain*. Filled with magnificent camera work and fun acted-out vignettes, the documentary is a real joy. The film's soundtrack includes such Prince tunes as "Little Red Corvette," "Play in the Sunshine," "Slow Love," "You Got the Look," "If I Was Your Girlfriend," and "The Cross."

In 1989, Prince returned to the forefront of the movie-going public's imagination with a number of songs he composed for Tim Burton's hit film *Batman*, including the song "Bat Dance," which featured samplings from Michael Keaton and Jack Nicholson's dialogue in the film.

Prince's *Batman* album was released with the caveat that the music was "inspired by the motion picture"—an inventive gambit oft-repeated since—which meant that Tim Burton did not feel obligated to use it as the soundtrack to his film, eventually scored by Danny Elfman.

But the Prince-Batman combination was a potent one, and the album sold some six million copies. The extended version of "Bat Dance" also got heavy play on radio stations nationwide, priming the pump for the summer's "Bat Fever" or "Bat Frenzy," as various people called it.

All of this good work was done with Magnoli's participation as Prince's new business manager, but soon thereafter the two men reached a permanent parting of the ways. Magnoli did not get to make *The Dawn*, and another project, *Graffiti Bridge*, was rushed into production in 1990.

Although billed as a pseudo-sequel to *Purple Rain* and featuring the welcome return of Morris Day and Jerome Benton, *Graffiti Bridge* was a straight-up musical, with characters singing to each other and breaking spontaneously into song. The film was also entirely studio-bound, featuring several artificial exterior sets, including the titular bridge, which gave the project a made-for-TV, almost claustrophobic feel.

In *Graffiti Bridge*, Morris Day and The Kid—played again by the film's director, Prince—are once again at creative and professional odds, this time over ownership of a nightclub called Grand Slam. It is the last club in town not owned exclusively by Morris Day, who is still a money-hungry villain, and who likes to hang out at the demonically named Pandemonium.

Involved in the dispute between The Kid and Morris is a woman, apparently an angel or muse, named Aura (Ingrid Chavez). Her presence, as well as the battle between a messianic Prince and a demonic Morris Day, suggests an overt spiritual approach, but like *Under the Cherry Moon*, the film seems to take itself far too seriously. A Prince without a sense of humor—remember Lake Minnetonka?—is almost insufferable to watch for any long duration.

Audiences seemed to agree, and—paling in comparison to Madonna's sensational *Truth or Dare* (1991)—Prince's "comeback" movie made less than $5 million at the box office. To date, *Graffiti Bridge* represents Prince's last directorial or starring turn in a movie.

The remarkable years since have seen Prince's career go up and down like a roller coaster. That he is talented is well documented and an entirely settled matter, yet his recent career has been marked by controversies and what—to an outsider, at least—seems strange, self-destructive behavior.

In 1993, upon turning thirty-five, Prince celebrated his emancipation from his previous benefactor, Warner Bros., by changing his name to a symbol.

Since this symbol is unpronounceable to the human tongue, the media far and wide disparagingly—and for years on end—referred to him as "The Artist Formerly Known as Prince." For many music fans, this change-in-name-to-a-symbol strategy made the Purple One something of a laughingstock.

After a while, Prince simply became known as "The Artist," which at least was better than a symbol. "The Artist" states what Prince is, and conveys something of his true nature: mercurial, sometimes commercial, but always gifted and pushing boundaries in his music.

As this book was written, Prince—once more going by that royal-sounding name—again ruffled audience feathers by imperiously declaring that "the Internet is completely over." Of course, this news came as a surprise to the 1,966,514,816 people around the globe who were still regularly using the Internet as of June 30, 2010.

Still, despite the fact that the Internet hosts over one quarter of the Earth's population, Prince refused to see his latest album, his twenty-seventh, released on any digital platform whatsoever. "I don't see why I should give my new music to iTunes or anyone else," he explained. "They won't pay me an advance for it and then they get angry when they can't get it."[31]

Once more, Prince's motives and behavior seem remarkably opaque. He's either way, way ahead of the technology curve and envisioning the next iteration of music appreciation or, fifty-two years old and a multimillionaire, finally, *deeply*, resolutely out of touch with his fans and the general population.

What's required at this juncture, perhaps, is a Magnoli-sponsored *Purple Rain 2*, a film that could reveal what ultimately became of that hurt, angry, but immensely appealing, talented and sympathetic Kid from Minneapolis. Did he wall himself off after becoming famous, growing eccentric and strange? Or did he stay in touch with his roots?

Perhaps in the event of such a film, the curtain on the method behind Prince's madness would be lifted once more, and we would all understand, forever, what makes this singular talent tick. But until that happens, *Purple Rain* remains the first and best "vision" of Prince available.

CHAPTER 4

It's Time We All Reach Out for Something New
Why *Purple Rain* Endures

As we gaze back at *Purple Rain* over twenty-five years later, the Magnoli film's greatest asset and strength remains its unshakable sense of authenticity: this notion that Prince—"The Kid"—may be a music star in the making or even a prodigy, but these qualities do not mean he's necessarily nice, or easy to get along with. There's nothing comfortable at all about this movie protagonist, and as viewers, we sense that's also true of the real Prince.

A conventional backstage musical or musical "rock" biography might play it safe in the manner of the *Purple Rain* contemporary, Rick Springfield vehicle *Hard to Hold*, transforming and packaging its upfront hero as some jovial, laughing, likeable stud. Or it might attempt to lionize its subject, its musician star, so that the audience lands firmly on his or her side during predictable second-act reversals and traumas.

Some modern musical biographies even go so far as to sand off the rough edges of their stars so as to make them more appealing to the moviegoing masses, easier to sell to the widest possible demographic range.

Albert Magnoli has seen this very process happen more than once, specifically in the case of two efforts that followed *Purple Rain* in the marketplace: *Cool as Ice* (1991), starring rap flame-out Vanilla Ice, and *8 Mile* (2002), starring legitimate phenomenon and talent Eminem.

"I'm friends with the director who made *Cool as Ice*. I knew what he was up against, and he knew what he was up against. He tried to make something authentic. You have to be careful," Magnoli explains. "*8 Mile* succeeded a lot more, but I was surprised at how soft that was.

"Let's be honest, if I [had been] given that material, the fact is that this kid is enraged. His lyrics are about rage. His whole upbringing was about being enraged and outraged, but there was no rage or outrage in that movie. That's what fueled everything else.

"I appreciated the movie, don't get me wrong," Magnoli clarifies. "It was very cool and very hip and did extremely well. But there was some kind of *homogenization* going on, which surprised me, given who was in control of that movie,

Brian Grazer, a very good producer. You had some serious talent there."

Magnoli considers himself fortunate he did not have to soft-pedal Prince's story to bring it to mass audiences. "It was never discussed. No one ever came to me and said, 'This is just too dark and too complicated; the character is too conflicted, the father's too evil, the audience isn't going to be sympathetic,'" he detailed.

"I wasn't making it PG-13. It had to be in their language: 'fuck, shit, bitch, damn.' These words had to be expressed, which threw us into an R rating. No one came at me over that. I was adamant from the beginning that this was R rated . . . unless it wasn't. But it wasn't going to be because I changed something," he emphasized.

And truthfully, flouting tradition, *Purple Rain* doesn't smooth over or whitewash any of The Kid's hard or uncomfortable edges. A child of an abusive father, he unwittingly continues the generational cycle of violence, unfortunately common in the culture he hails from.

In one horrifying instance, he backhands Apollonia, and it seems vicious. Movies don't show us this kind of behavior anymore, especially not from people who are supposed to be "likeable." This is an act The Kid immediately regrets, but it happens nonetheless. We understand the behavior, yet it still feels abhorrent and wrong.

Similarly, The Kid is depicted as overcontrolling and self-obsessed with his talent, with his music. He refuses even just to listen to the song written by his Revolution bandmates, Wendy and Lisa.

Artistically, The Kid can be downright cruel, as we see in his performance of the scandalous "Darling Nikki," and also remote, cerebral, and noncommercial, as during his performance of "Computer Blue."

Impressively, *Purple Rain* emphasizes these personal traits—ostensibly Prince's real-life personality traits—and implies in no small way, through compositions such as "When Doves Cry," that for The Kid to succeed, he must overcome these demons.

Accordingly, the film's most emotional and important moment occurs when The Kid lets go; when he stops holding on to everything so damn tightly. Finally, he positions his father's legacy in his *now*, in his present (as a troubled, but altogether human man, thus worthy of sympathy despite his misdeeds), and performs Wendy and Lisa's song, "Purple Rain," which he did not create.

For someone who, in the words of that scoundrel and dandy Morris Day, "never did anything for anyone else," this is no small matter. At the very least, it's a start: a clean break from the past.

Purple Rain succeeds because it reveals The Kid, warts and all, and presents a picture of a talent who is amazing yet, like so many of us, also has a lot of personal baggage to overcome. I can't say that many rock biographies feel this human, or this real. But Prince isn't just dour or violent in the film either; the approach allows glimpses of his wicked sense of humor and his sexual charisma too. It's a fully dimensional glimpse of the artist.

Magnoli's film also remains particularly admirable as a rock opera of the musical genre. Although the characters don't actually sing lyrics as dialogue to one another in the body of the film, the movie nonetheless conforms to the tradition of the format: *the right song at the right time and place in the narrative.*

In other words, Prince's brilliant songs and compositions, carefully selected for the film by the director himself, tell much of the story. The songs reflect the thematic, narrative content. Again, this is an approach that many rock biographies eschew, to their jeopardy.

Specifically, "Let's Go Crazy" opens the film and serves two distinct purposes. First, it makes clear in lyrics that the movie will concern this mystery "we call life," an acknowledgment of the film's multidimensional approach to its star.

Second, the idea inherent in the title, of "going crazy," combined with the invitation "let's," makes the audience aware that the movie is going to show us this "life" in a manner we have not seen before in our culture. The movie goes crazy in terms of style, in terms of fashion, in terms of our sense of conventional movie decorum and tradition. The music video age is here.

During "Let's Go Crazy," the movie purposely fractures time and space with its fast-cutting montage of various characters preparing for the show at the First Avenue Club: applying eyeliner, riding in a taxi, even dressing before a mirror. The cumulative effect of the rousing song (again, essentially an invitation) and the preparatory images is an unbounded sense of enthusiasm and anticipation.

"Darling Nikki" is another song that echoes for the viewers the details of the narrative. With Apollonia in the audience, The Kid performs, singing of a "sex fiend" named Nikki, one who asks him to sign "on the dotted line," suggesting a Faustian bargain of sorts, a contract at the least.

The implication is that Apollonia is analogous to the proverbial Nikki, a slut or sex fiend with ulterior, money-grubbing motives. The scene is lensed in a lurid red light, with The Kid humping, bumping, and grinding onstage—all the while shirtless and perspiring. We understand immediately why Apollonia should be hurt. This song is no less than a frontal assault: an attack and dismissal.

Other tunes perform a similar thematic function in the narrative. The early "Take Me with U," of course, is a joyous love song, concerning the auspicious beginnings of a new romantic relationship. It is playful, upbeat, and brimming with the joy of possibilities, like the start of any great romance. The "dark clouds" have not entered the picture yet when "Take Me with U" plays, and it stands in stark contrast to the later, vicious stylings of "Darling Nikki."

"Sex Shooter" by Apollonia 6 and "Jungle Love" by Morris Day and the Time, while beautifully performed and infinitely memorable (so much so that Kevin Smith revived the latter for a loving tribute in 2001's *Jay and Silent Bob Strike Back*), are nonetheless indications that The Kid is the real artist in town, and thus the one deserving of a slot at the club.

By contrast, Morris Day and Apollonia are unapologetically not artists. Rather, they are all about "making it." Their music is seamlessly entertaining but not high art; not representative of deeply held or expressed feelings of "self."

In these tunes, as well as "The Bird"—a deliberate "Jungle Love" sound-alike or knock-off—*Purple Rain* seems to get at the way that bands and musicians package themselves as brand names without really being about anything beyond lacy lingerie, zoot suits, and syncopated dance moves.

Not that there's anything wrong or ignoble about simply entertaining an audience. But these "packaged" numbers are designed and meant as a strong contrast to the traumatic, heartfelt music of a talent like The Kid, which can be used as a bludgeon ("Darling Nikki") or as a crucible for self-reflection ("When Doves Cry").

Written specifically for the film, "When Doves Cry" arrives as The Kid is at his lowest ebb. His father has attempted suicide. His girlfriend has been seduced by promises of fame from Morris Day and Jerome Benton. His bandmates, particularly Wendy and Lisa, are estranged because he won't try out their song . . . or even listen to it. Finally, Billy Sparks is ready to oust The Kid and the Revolution from the First Avenue Club, meaning that very shortly, The Kid might have no audience.

Like his father, then, he will be relegated to a home studio, to a piano in the living room, living with only memories and regret. Those emotions will give way to violence and anger. It's a slippery slope.

The lyrics of "When Doves Cry" establish that The Kid may be just like his father and mother—in other words, a failure in life. The lyrics suggest that he is doomed, through the cycle of domestic violence, to repeat their mistakes, personally and professionally.

The visual montage that accompanies the song reveals The Kid on his motorcycle on the open road, choosing which path to take, which to avoid. Again, it is the perfect marriage of imagery and audio, telling audiences everything they need to know about The Kid, about his dilemma and existential crisis at this point in the film.

Finally, there is "Purple Rain," the movie's title song. It is a gorgeous, almost religious composition that has been termed a celebration of woman (related to the menstrual cycle) and both an apology for bad behavior and a promise of sexual ecstasy, according to some critics, such as David Denby.

The color purple has long been associated with creativity, dignity, and wisdom, all qualities that The Kid has in abundance, if only he can tap into them. Rain, of course, is cleansing. Rain is also sometimes heralded as a fertilizing agent, a downpour that suggests a new way of life.

Thus the purple (dignity, wisdom, creativity) rain (cleansing, birthing agent) represents the spiritual rebirth of The Kid. Also encoded in the notion of purple rain is a kind of spiritual forgiveness—-the hard anger of "red" softened, perhaps.

Without ever seeming obvious or trite, the music and imagery in *Purple Rain* always help the audience feel the right emotion at exactly the right time to fully enjoy and appreciate the tale: excitement ("Let's Go Crazy"), anger and betrayal ("Darling Nikki"), indecision and personal reflection ("When Doves Cry"), and finally, an almost spiritual, orgiastic release, rebirth, and sense of redemption ("Purple Rain").

Each song thus represents an important step on The Kid's journey to adulthood and on to stardom, a destination acknowledged in the film's final valediction, "Baby I'm a Star." You can't get there unless you know who you are and where you've been, and the film's imagery and songs lead the viewer to that realization, that conclusion in beautiful, clever, and effective fashion.

This was all intentional. Magnoli learned at USC the balance between maintaining artistic vision and the demands of popular, commercial film.

"How do you create commercial product that attracts an audience but at the same time hold on to that which put you in the room in the first place?" he asks rhetorically. "When you forget how, you fail. When you remember, you win. That axiom defines those who are successful in this town and those who aren't."

Purple Rain endures in the twenty-first century because it does exactly what some studio executives might have imagined impossible. It takes a half-Italian, half–African American, short Minneapolis rock star and instead of turning him into an icon by downplaying his contradictions, reveals them in all their magnificent humanity. *Right there . . . at center stage.*

The Kid, and by extension, Prince, is a man of encroaching "dark clouds," as Wendy and Lisa indicate, but strangely, this worrisome admission about the man and his musical genius makes him all the more approachable, all the more laudable for his amazing accomplishments.

Purple Rain stylishly and emotionally provides audiences the best glimpse of Prince we've ever had, and chronicles the life and times of an artist in conflict . . . and yet at the top of his game.

NOTES

Chapter 1. Baby I'm a Star

1. Gary Graff, "Prince: Money's One Thing, Soul Another," *The Charlotte Observer,* December 31, 1987, 19A.

2. Seth Colter Walls, "Pop's Virtual Royalty—Prince Once Ruled the Web. Now He's Got to Step It Up," *Newsweek,* March 23, 2009, 57.

3. Andrew Kopkind, *The Nation*, September 22, 1984, 252.

4. Bonnie Allen, "It's Raining Prince," *Essence*, November 1984, 56.

5. Nicholas Jennings, "A Black star blazes in pop's heavens," *MacLean's*, December 3, 1984, 70.

6. Barbara Graustark, "Prince's Purple Reign," *People Magazine* 22, no. 21 (November 19, 1984), 161.

7. Trudy S. Moore, "Prince Makes Debut as Actor in His Hot Film, *Purple Rain*," *Jet*, August 27, 1984, 46–48.

8. Lynn Norment, "Prince: The Story Behind the Passion for Purple and Privacy," *Ebony*, November 1, 1985, 67–74.

9. Brian Morton, *Prince: A Thief in the Temple* (New York: Canongate Books, 2007), 95.

10. David Denby, "Dr. Feelgood," *New York Magazine*, August 13, 1984, 51–52.

11. Sam Stall, Lou Harry, and Julia Spalding, *The Encyclopedia of Guilty Pleasures* (San Francisco: Quirk Books, 2004), 215.

Chapter 3. I Want Some Perfection

1. Per Nilsen, *Dance Music Sex Romance: Prince: The First Decade* (London: Firefly Publishing, 1999), 21.

2. Martin Charles Strong, *The Essential Rock Discography* (Edinburgh: Canongate Books, 2006), 858.

3. CNN.Com, "Prince," http://archives.cnn.com/1999 /SHOWBIZ/Music/12/20/wb.prince.bio/.

4. Peter Buckley, *The Rough Guide to Rock* (New York: Penguin Group, 2003), vii.

5. Nilsen, *Dance Music Sex Romance*, 144.

6. Nilsen, *Dance Music Sex Romance*, 144.

7. Matthew Carcieri, *Prince: A Life in Music* (Lincoln: iUniverse, 2004), 23.

8. Brian Raftery, "*Purple Rain*, The Oral History," *Spin Magazine*, July 2009, 54.

9. Internet Movie Database, http://www.imdb.com/name/nm0536299/bio.

10. R. Serge Denisoff and William D. Romanowski, *Risky Business: Rock in Film,* 1990 (New Brunswick: Transaction Publishers, 1991), 440.

11. John Waterhouse, "Time Marches on for Frontman Morris Day," *Access Atlanta/Music in Atlanta,* July 17, 2009, http://accessatlanta.com/atlanta-music/time-marches-on-for-92371.html.

12. "Entertainment: Michael Jackson Pens Major Film Deal with Geffen Movie Company," *Jet,* November 26, 1984, 56.

13. Bob Gulla, *Icons of R&B and Soul: An Encyclopedia of Artists Who Revolutionized Rhythm* (Westport: Greenwood Press, 2008), 489.

14. Stephen Prince, *A New Pot of Gold: Hollywood Under the Electric Rainbow, 1980–1989* (Berkeley: University of California Press, 2002), 135.

15. John Nangle, *Films in Review,* October 1984, 496.

16. Sheila Benson, *The Los Angeles Times,* July 27, 1984, Calendar, 1.

17. Andrew Kopkind, *The Nation,* September 22, 1984, 251.

18. Eloise Salholz and Linda Tibbetts, "Getting the Prince Look," *Newsweek,* October 1, 1985, 84.

19. Rob Nelson, "The Color Purple," *Arts & Entertainment, Minneapolis & St. Paul,* http://www.mspmag.com/entertainment/film/151742_1.asp.

20. Wayne Robins, *Newsday,* July 27, 1984, 2, 9.

21. James Wolcott, "Prince of Wails," *Texas Monthly,* September 1984, 180.

22. Michael Shore, "The Prince Interview. Mr. Purple Discusses His Movies, His Music, His Musicians And More, More, More," *Rock & Soul,* April 1986, http://princetext.tripod.com/i_mtv85.html

23. David Denby, *New York Magazine,* August 13, 1984, 50.

24. Janice Delaney, Mary Jane Lupton, and Emily Toth, *The Curse: A Cultural History of Menstruation* (Urbana: University of Illinois Press, 1988), 158.

25. Kenya N. Byrd, "Flashback Fridays: Morris Day," *Essence.com,* July 30, 2009, www.1.essence.com/news_entertainment/entertainment/articles/flashback_fridays_morris_day/.

26. Priya Elan, "Purple Reign," *The Guardian,* September 20, 2008, http://www.guardian.co.uk/music/2008/sep/20/1.

27. Jeff Borden, "It All Started with *Purple Rain,*" *The Charlotte Observer,* July 2, 1989, 2F.

28. Alvin F. Pouissaint, M.D., "An Analytical Look at the Prince Phenomenon," *Ebony,* June 1985, 170.

29. Pauline Kael, *State of the Art* (New York: Maryion Boyars, 1985), 213.

30. Joann Rhetts, "*Under the Cherry Moon* Shows Prince Still Has Whey with Words," *The Charlotte Observer*, July 4, 1986, 6F.

31. Emma Barnett, "Prince: The Internet's Completely Over," *The Telegraph*, July 6, 2010, http://www.telegraph .co.uk/technology/news/7874307/Prince-the-internets -completely-over.html.

SELECTED BIBLIOGRAPHY

Buckley, Peter. *The Rough Guide to Rock*. New York: Penguin Group, 2003.

Carcieri, Matthew. *Prince: A Life in Music*. Lincoln: iUniverse, 2004

Gulla, Bob. *Icons of R&B and Soul: An Encyclopedia of Artists Who Revolutionized Rhythm*. Westport: Greenwood Press, 2008.

Morton, Brian. *Prince: A Thief in the Temple*. New York: Canongate Books, 2007.

Muir, John Kenneth. *The Rock and Roll Film Encyclopedia*. New York: Applause Theatre and Cinema Books, 2007.

Nilsen, Per. *Dance Music Sex Romance: Prince: The First Decade*. London: Firefly Publishing, 1999.

Prince, Stephen. *A New Pot of Gold: Hollywood Under the Electric Rainbow, 1980–1989.* Berkeley: University of California Press, 2002.

Strong, Martin Charles. *The Essential Rock Discography.* Edinburgh: Canongate Books, 2006.

INDEX

MUSIC ON FILM

A Hard Day's Night
by Ray Morton
Paperback • 4.75" x 6.5"
8 page color photo insert
978-0-87910-388-0
$9.99

Amadeus
by Ray Morton
Paperback • 4.75" x 6.5"
8 page color photo insert
978-0-87910-381-1
$9.99

Purple Rain
by John Kenneth Muir
Paperback • 4.75" x 6.5"
8 page color photo insert
978-0-87910-396-5
$9.99

The Rocky Horror Picture Show
by Dave Thompson
Paperback • 4.75" x 6.5"
8 page color photo insert
978-0-87910-387-3
$9.99

Each book in the series highlights one musical film from every angle, with features such as rarely seen color photos, notes on the origins of the film, behind-the-scenes stories of the making of the film, critics' and audience's reactions to the film, and much more.

Cabaret
by Stephen Tropiano
Paperback • 4.75" x 6.5"
8 page color photo insert
978-0-87910-382-8
$9.99

Grease
by Stephen Tropiano
Paperback • 4.75" x 6.5"
8 page color photo insert
978-0-87910-389-7
$9.99

This Is Spinal Tap
by John Kenneth Muir
Paperback • 4.75" x 6.5"
8 page color photo insert
978-0-87910-377-4
$12.99

West Side Story
by Barry Monush
Paperback • 4.75" x 6.5"
8 page color photo insert
978-0-87910-378-1
$12.99